Beyond the Sanctuary

Essays on Liturgy, Life, and Discipleship

Timothy A. Johnston
Editor

Nihil Obstat
Rev. Mr. Daniel G. Welter, JD
Chancellor
Archdiocese of Chicago
April 17, 2020

Imprimatur
Most Rev. Ronald A. Hicks
Vicar General
Archdiocese of Chicago
April 17, 2020

The *Nihil Obstat* and *Imprimatur* are declarations that the material is free from doctrinal or moral error, and thus is granted permission to publish in accordance with c. 827. No legal responsibility is assumed by the grant of this permission. No implication is contained herein that those who have granted the *Nihil Obstat* and *Imprimatur* agree with the content, opinions, or statements expressed.

This book was edited by Timothy A. Johnston. Christian Rocha was the production editor, Juan Alberto Castillo was the designer, and Luis Leal was the production artist.

Cover art by Anthony Ward.

24 23 22 21 20   1 2 3 4 5

Printed in the United States of America

Library of Congress Control Number: 2020936469

ISBN 978-1-61671-530-4

BSC

CONTENTS

PREFACE

For you shall go to all to whom I send you,
and you shall speak whatever I command you.
—Jeremiah 1:7

As a young boy, I was enamored with the celebration of the liturgy. From week to week, my imagination was captured by the singing assembly, the Scripture stories proclaimed, and the prayerful manner our pastor prayed the Eucharist Prayer. Of course, I did not know what it all meant at the time, but because the liturgy was prepared and celebrated well (and my family was actively engaged), I fell in love with it and it shaped me. Without knowing it, I was being formed in the paschal mystery of Christ, learning a rhythm of how to be Christian in the world.

After college, I decided to study the Church's liturgy with the hope of accompanying others as they grew to know Christ more deeply through the liturgy. In my professional ministry, I have witnessed the transformative power of the liturgy numerous times. For example, while a campus minister at Marquette University, students helped me understand the real connection between the liturgy celebrated and the liturgy lived. I watched Matt and Justin welcome a homeless man to sit next them at Mass and then share dinner with him; I accompanied students to the March for Life and saw how the Eucharist motivated them to serve all God's people; I listened to students who fed the hungry in Milwaukee and volunteered at shelters for abused women and children. A faith nurtured in the Church's liturgy made these profound, yet simple encounters possible.

Beyond the Sanctuary: Liturgy, Life, and Discipleship is a collection of essays that invites the reader to discover how the liturgy transforms the worshiping assembly and sends it on mission. There is an intimate relationship between the liturgy and our daily lives. Pope Francis says in *Evangelii gaudium*, "The joy of the Gospel fills the hearts and lives of all who encounter Jesus" (1). The Christ we encounter at the liturgy is the Joy we are called to share "to the ends of the earth" (Acts 1:8). Pope John Paul II says it this way: "Receiving the bread of life, the disciples of Christ ready themselves to undertake with the strength of the Risen Lord and his Spirit the tasks which await them in their ordinary life" (*Dies Domini*, 45). Like the prophet Jeremiah, we too are called and sent.

The themes in this resource were initially developed as Track 3 of *The Essentials of Catholic Liturgy* course developed by Liturgy Training Publications in partnership with the National Association of Pastoral Musicians. During the development, it became clear that a pastoral resource that explores these topics was necessary to help the faithful understand how the liturgy forms us, sends us forth on mission, and draws us back to be nourished in Word and sacrament. As you read these essays, take time to contemplate how the liturgy has shaped you and the community of believers. To whom is God sending you to share the Good News?

Timothy A. Johnston, editor
December 14, 2019
Memorial of St. John of the Cross

ABBREVIATIONS

AA — *Apostolicam actuositatem*, Vatican II, "Decree on the Apostolate of the Laity," 1965

AG — *Ad gentes*, Vatican II, "Decree on the Church's Missionary Activity," 1965

CCC — *Catechism of the Catholic Church*

CSD — *Compendium of the Social Doctrine of the Church*, Pontifical Council for Peace and Justice, English trans. USCCB, 2005

DD — *Dies Domini*, John Paul II, "On Keeping the Lord's Day Holy," 1998

EG — *Evangelii gaudium*, Francis, "The Joy of the Gospel," 2013

EJA — *Economic Justice for All: Pastoral Letter on Catholic Social Teaching and the US Economy*, USCCB, 1986

EN — *Evangelii nuntiandi*, Paul VI, "Evangelization in the Modern World," 1975

GDC — *General Directory for Catechesis*, Congregation for the Clergy, 1998

GIRM — ICEL translation of *Institutio Generalis Missalis Romani*, 2002, the promulgated form of the fifth edition of this instruction, incorporating adaptations approved for dioceses of the United States

GMD — *Go and Make Disciples: A National Plan and Strategy for Catholic Evangelization in the United States*, USCCB, 2002

GS — *Gaudium et spes*, Vatican II, "Pastoral Constitution on the Church in the Modern World," 1965

ICEL — International Commission on English in the Liturgy

IJ — *Institutiones Justiniani*, codified by Justinian I, "Institutes of Justinian," sixth century

LG — *Lumen gentium*, Vatican II, "Dogmatic Constitution on the Church," 1964

OBC	*Order of Baptism of Children*, ICEL, 2019
OCF	*Order of Christian Funerals*, ICEL, 1988
OM	Order of Mass
QA	*Quadragesimo anno*, Pius XI, "In the 40th Year: Reconstruction of the Social Order," 1931
RCIA	*Rite of Christian Initiation of Adults*, 1988
RM	*Missale Romanum*, editio typica tertia, "The Third Edition of the Roman Missal," 2011
SacCar	*Sacramentum caritatis*, Benedict XVI, "The Sacrament of Charity," 2007
SC	*Sacrosanctum concilium*, Vatican II, "Constitution on the Sacred Liturgy," 1963
STL	*Sing to the Lord: Music in Divine Worship*, USCCB, 2007
USCCB	United States Conference of Catholic Bishops

1 Liturgy, Life, and Discipleship

ANNE McGOWAN

Baptism creates Christians and bestows our fundamental identity as liturgists. The Second Vatican Council's *Sacrosanctum concilium* (SC) promotes "full, conscious, and active" participation, "which is demanded by the very nature of the liturgy, and to which the Christian people . . . have a right and to which they are bound by reason of their Baptism" (SC, 14). Therefore, every Christian has a liturgical ministry, even if this ministry is exercised by most, through their participation as members of the assembly—from the tiniest child focusing on the interplay of light, shadow, and people in a passing procession to the elderly woman with dementia whose body now bears the majority of her most conscious liturgical memories as she springs to full attention for the communal recitation of the Lord's Prayer and the reception of communion. Every Christian is likewise shaped by the pattern of Christ's dying and rising presented in the liturgy and thus lives, consciously or unconsciously, out of a liturgical spirituality. In Baptism, we are marked with the sign of the cross and claimed for Christ.[1] This identification with Christ is initially inscribed on our bodies, revived even by occasional liturgical engagement, and invigorated by regular and consistent liturgical practice. Embodied liturgical participation enables us to claim and rehearse our Christian identity. From that

1. The sign of the cross is administered either at the beginning of the baptismal rite (infant to around six years) or during the Rite of Acceptance into the Order of Catechumens (seven years through adulthood).

perspective, we can start to experience the world differently, recognizing and receiving the ability to discern God's presence and activity in the objects, places, people, relationships, and events in our world as it is and as it might become. Rooted now in this experiential identity, we become better equipped to discern our response to God's call and enact it as missionary disciples.

Several theological principles reemphasized in the documents of Vatican II and since restored to greater prominence in liturgical celebrations, ground the practice of all ministry and missionary activity in the Church, including lay ministry. Baptism is emphasized repeatedly as the foundation of all ministry, as in *Apostolicam actuositatem* (AA):

> Lay people's right and duty to be apostles derives from their union with Christ their head. Inserted as they are in the mystical body of Christ by baptism and strengthened in the power of the holy Spirit in confirmation, it is by the Lord himself that they are assigned to the apostolate. . . . Charity, which is, as it were, the soul of the whole apostolate, is given to them and nourished in them by the sacraments, and especially by the Eucharist. (3)

Liturgical reforms have fostered a "warm and lively appreciation of sacred scripture" and "a richer fare [has been] provided for the faithful at the table of God's word" (SC, 24, 51). Certainly, all of the Church's ministers need to be steeped in God's Word as it is handed on and interpreted through the Church's tradition in the course of the liturgical year. Furthermore, Vatican II encouraged all Christians to reclaim their identity as full participants in the Church's liturgies, especially the Eucharistic liturgy, which is identified as the "source and summit" not just of the Church's liturgies but also of Christian life (see SC, 10, *Lumen gentium,* 11). As the repeatable sacrament of initiation, the regular sacrament of healing, and a source of strength for sacraments of service, the Eucharistic liturgy presents a pattern for appropriating Christ's paschal mystery so that we might serve God with humility and joy, enlivened by the Holy Spirit.

Liturgy as God's Gift to Us

Liturgy is "the work of the people"—understood in a very particular way. When the Christian community adopted *leitourgia,* a secular Greek term for public work on behalf of people, the paradigmatic reference was to the work of Christ undertaken for us and for our salvation. As members of Christ's body and sharers in his Spirit, we become able to participate in God's ongoing saving mission for the life of the world as it unfolds in historical time and will be fully realized in eternity.

> The mystery we're trying to celebrate in liturgy is the fact that Jesus Christ died and rose for our salvation, and we have died and risen through Baptism to new life in him. That life is expressed in the liturgy. It is nourished through scripture and the Eucharist and prayer. . . . Our liturgy is God's gift to us, not ours to [God].[2]

The fact that liturgy is for us and not something God needs from us is expressed well in one of the options for the introductory portion of the Eucharistic Prayer: "our thanksgiving is itself your [i.e., God's] gift, / since our praises add nothing to your greatness / but profit us for salvation" (*Roman Missal,* Common Preface IV).

Ideally, public worship is a primary source of theological encounter for baptized Christians. It is also formational insofar as much of what we learn about Christian discipleship we can grasp explicitly or implicitly through the rituals of worship or subsequent reflection upon them, or both. Such insights can come from the words of the liturgy and its prayers, from the symbols that surround us, or from the welcome of a friend or stranger who shows us something of the hospitality of God. Therefore, the quality of liturgical celebrations should not be an afterthought since the faith of people may be at stake, as the US bishops have observed: "Good celebrations can foster and nourish faith. Poor celebrations may weaken it" (*Sing to the Lord*, 5).

In the Introductory Rites of the Mass, for example, we "become" the Church, the assembled people of God. We gather with

2. Bryan Cones and Robert Taft, "Mass Instruction: Fr. Robert Taft on Liturgical Reform," *U.S. Catholic* 74, no. 12 (December 2009): 29.

people we might not otherwise choose to associate with—who are holy people God chose and called together. We come bringing nothing less than ourselves and the "joys and hopes, the grief and anguish" of our lives and our world (*Gaudium et spes*, 1), which is all that we have to offer God. As the Mass begins, one of the first collective acts is signing ourselves again with the cross in the name of the Triune God. This reminds us that our fundamental identity is now in Christ—and that we do not get to engage the liturgy entirely on our own terms. We experience Christ already present with us in the presider and the praying, singing assembly and prepare to encounter Christ in the Scriptures and the Sacrament of the Eucharist (SC, 7).

In the Liturgy of the Word, we are invited to listen in, ultimately to let God sanctify our lives and the life of the world. God presents us with God's own life-giving words, now "enfleshed" again in a new proclamation. These words have the power to change us and are offered out of a love that does not want us to remain as we are. These words are given to draw us into closer relationship with God, through Christ, in the power of the Holy Spirit—and with everyone else whom God also loved into existence and with all of creation. God stands eager to help facilitate these connections for us, opening a vision for a new way of life. At times, we can hear the Word of God and feel illuminated to enter more deeply into the good work that God has already begun for us in our lives, our many communities, and our world. At other times, we might feel stung and challenged because God's Word calls us to change—and change is difficult. Preaching done well can lead us to further insights into what God's Word means for our lives in the world today—including our specific time and place and cultural setting. With the general intercessions, we are invited to prayerfully explore how God's Word might be leading us into mission. The *General Instruction of the Roman Missal* notes:

> In the Universal Prayer or Prayer of the Faithful, the people respond in some sense to the Word of God which they have received in faith and, exercising the office of their baptismal Priesthood, offer prayers to God for the salvation of all. (GIRM, 69)

These prayers ideally involve the meeting of God's Word appointed for proclamation (drawing on the language and imagery of the lectionary readings) and the world as it is when the local community gathers to celebrate.

The Liturgy of the Eucharist draws us more fully toward mission. We begin by bringing ourselves and what little we have before God who needs none of it so that we can become people who know in our bones that "it is right and just" to give God thanks and praise. The Eucharistic Prayers contain language that helps us imagine and live into connections between liturgy and life. For example:

> Look, O Lord, upon the Sacrifice / which you yourself have provided for your Church, / and grant in your loving kindness / to all who partake of this one Bread and one Chalice / that, gathered into one body by the Holy Spirit, / they may truly become a living sacrifice in Christ / to the praise of your glory. (*The Roman Missal*, Eucharistic Prayer IV)

> Open our eyes / to the needs of our brothers and sisters; / inspire in us words and actions / to comfort those who labor and are burdened. / Make us serve them truly, / after the example of Christ and at his command. / And may your Church stand as a living witness / to truth and freedom, / to peace and justice, / that all people may be raised up to a new hope. (*The Roman Missal*, Eucharistic Prayer for Various Needs IV)

Receiving communion is the fullest symbol of our participation in the Eucharistic liturgy that is the source and summit of our life of faith. The most profound Eucharistic miracle is not that bread and wine are transformed, but that we are transformed. We consume the Eucharistic body (and blood) of Christ so that we might become more fully what and who we already are as the ecclesial Body of Christ.

The Concluding Rites of the Mass are very brief, but include the portion of the liturgy where we are formally commissioned to go and continue what we have already begun to do in the liturgy. We may not feel quite ready yet to live out the implications of what we have said and done in the liturgy, but we are as ready as we ever will be to be sent out on mission. The Prayer after Communion and dismissal already suggest that the work of communion is not complete with the liturgical celebration. Although the Prayer after

Communion, concluding the Liturgy of the Eucharist, speaks more often of our heavenly hopes in relation to the communion we have just shared, it occasionally emphasizes our earthly responsibilities as on the Twenty-Second Sunday in Ordinary Time:

> Renewed by this bread from the heavenly table,
> we beseech you, Lord,
> that, being the food of charity,
> it may confirm our hearts
> and stir us to serve you in our neighbor. (*The Roman Missal*)

Before we can share God's gifts with others though, we need to really receive them ourselves, a process that leads us from life to liturgy and back again.

Learning to Live Sacramentally

Liturgy sanctifies through "symbols perceptible by the senses" (SC, 7, see also SC, 21, 33–34). We can recognize and receive God's gifts to us in the Church's sacraments in part because they rely on primary symbols like water, oil, fire, and bread that already have meaning for us from everyday life. We already experience water in our world as a cleansing, purifying, life-giving, and death-dealing substance—which helps us engage Baptism as our rebirth to new life in Christ and our sharing in Christ's death and Resurrection. We experience bread and wine as consumables that nourish and delight us and meal sharing as an act which can unite and reconcile those invited to the table and expose systematic injustice toward those excluded from the table. This helps us understand Eucharist simultaneously as meal and sacrifice that unites us to Christ, makes us more like him as we "become" what we eat, and calls us to become sustenance for others as we share our gifts and our faith.

Christ and the Church provide additional levels of sacramental mediation between the natural and cultural sacraments of everyday life and the Church's official ritual sacraments. Christ is a sacrament of God (insofar as, in his humanity, he made God and God's saving will visible to the world in a way that would not have been possible had the Incarnation not happened). Similarly, between Christ's Ascension into heaven and his coming again in glory, the Church is a sacrament of Christ as Christ's visible body in our world. *Lumen gentium* (LG) famously used this language: "the church, in Christ, is a sacrament—a sign and instrumen . . . of communion with God and of the unity of the entire human race" (LG, 1). Key markers of Christian identity like the Scriptures, sacraments, and ethics (i.e., behavior manifesting Christian discipleship) are mediated by the Church insofar as Christ's Body, the Church, has been entrusted with the *traditio*, or handing on, of these treasures of Christian faith and witness from one generation to the next as living realities.[3] God works in the lives of human persons in many ways, most of which remain a mystery to us, but the rites of the Church, like the Eucharist, help make some aspects of God's work more visible in the world.

All this makes possible a way of living in the world that is broadly sacramental and Eucharistic. Everyday objects, encounters, and relationships can become for us more than what they already are on a sensible level, now revelatory of the invisible Triune God and our relationship with this God. They can become "matter" for our Eucharist, our thanksgiving offered to God as a sacrifice of praise. We recognize that we are in a world full of signs and sacraments that God uses to communicate with us out of an abundance of grace, mercy, and love. In our gratitude, we discover joy and "find" God who was already there all along. It is from this perspective that the Church's Eucharist can really function as source and summit of Christian life.

Going Forth to Love and Serve

If the most profound Eucharistic transformation happens in us, what we do after the liturgy is just as important for us and for our salvation as what we do during it. Faith professed but not lived, as if "religion were nothing more than the fulfilment of acts of worship and the observance of a few moral obligations" (GS, 43), is insufficient. With what has been variously called the liturgy of the neighbor, liturgy of the world, and liturgy after the liturgy, we are finally in a

3. See Louis-Marie Chauvet, *The Sacraments: The Word of God at the Mercy of the Body*, trans. Madeleine Beaumont (Collegeville, MN: Liturgical Press, 2001).

position to offer a "return-gift" to God.[4] Our praise and thanksgiving coalesces into specific, visible responses to God's presence and "presents." We "verify" our love of God through love of neighbor and service to the world, continuing our Eucharistic ministry now as embodied sacraments who bear the presence of Christ to a hungry and fragmented world.

Liturgy broadly understood thus provides the foundation for discipleship, mission, and ministry, although the particular forms this takes will vary according to the myriad contexts and cultures in which local churches are situated, the concrete needs of creation and communities that present themselves in our evolving world, and the convergence of God's very particular callings for individuals and their cooperative and co-creative responses. Liturgy "in harmony with the character of the people" promotes the missionary activity of the Church when it helps local assemblies "daily become more conscious of themselves as living communities of faith, liturgy and charity" (*Ad gentes*, 19). The Church's liturgies, and especially our repeated participation in the Eucharistic liturgy throughout life, begin to remake us into a certain sort of people emboldened to be heralds and witnesses of the reign of God. Lived liturgy (*lex vivendi*) is thus compelling insofar as it leads those not yet connected with the visible Church to associate with worldly "liturgists," perhaps sensing some nascent attraction toward this Eucharistic way of life. To encounter sacramental Christians is to experience the ongoing work of Christ in the Church.

Liturgy that leads us into life will also lead us back to liturgy. "For the goal of apostolic endeavor is that all who are made children of God by faith and Baptism should come together to praise God in the midst of [God's] church, to take part in the sacrifice and to eat the Lord's Supper" (SC, 10). Our Eucharistic worship on earth is presented as an "appetizer" of the worship that, God willing, we will be doing forever when God's people are gathered for the heavenly banquet. To prepare us for full participation in that liturgy of everlasting life, we can hope that our approach to earthly liturgies might be active without prioritizing activity over contemplation, conscious without privileging intellectual comprehension (lest young baptized

4. Chauvet, 117–127.

children and people with cognitive challenges be excluded from claiming their rightful role as liturgists), and full in a way that is satisfied with nothing less than total commitment of our whole lives to God.

Questions for Discussion:

1. Reflect on your role as a liturgist commissioned by your Baptism. How does your status as a liturgist inform your identity and actions as a Christian and as a pastoral minister?
2. What practical steps could you take before, during, and after a liturgy to facilitate your own full, conscious, and active participation in the liturgy? How could you model full, conscious, and active liturgical participation for others and promote it in your ministry?
3. How has your past participation in liturgy formed you for Christian living and missionary discipleship? (Consider general principles and practices that have been significant for you over time as well as particular experiences that had a lasting impact.) How might you more consciously connect liturgy, life, and discipleship in the future?

2 Liturgy and the Modern World

KATHARINE E. HARMON

Introduction

Preaching in eighth-century ancient Israel, the prophet Amos announced the Lord's frustration with the people's worship:

> I hate, I despise your festivals, and I take no delight in your solemn assemblies. Even though you offer me your burnt offerings and grain offerings, I will not accept them; and the offerings of well-being of your fatted animals I will not look upon. Take away from me the noise of your songs; I will not listen to the melody of your harps. But let justice roll down like waters, and righteousness like an ever-flowing stream. (Amos 5:21–24)

For Amos, worship of God without love of neighbor was nothing more than a clanging gong or a clashing cymbal. True life in God could not separate love of God and love of neighbor. Likewise, Jesus affirmed this in his own recounting of the "most important" commandment to a group of questioning Pharisees:

> "You shall love the Lord your God with all your heart, and with all your soul, and with all your mind." This is the greatest and first commandment. And a second is like it: "You shall love your neighbor as yourself." On these two commandments hang all the law and the prophets. (Matthew 22:37–40)

Yet, the essential connection between liturgy and justice, so readily apparent in salvation history, is challenging to articulate in our contemporary Church. How, exactly, are we to understand the Mass as illustrating an awareness of the challenges of the modern world? Should we rely on our petitions to respond to pressing concerns of the community that week? Should our pastor address a difficult current event in his homily? Should the announcements advertise a social outreach organization like St. Vincent de Paul? Even more problematically, how does one speak about issues of "justice" that are so easily politicized in an American context—questions of gun control, immigration, or climate change, to name a few? What is "just" seems to change based upon one's political affiliation, or even upon whether one identifies as a "progressive" or "traditionalist" Catholic!

Interpreting how the liturgy might respond to the needs of the modern world requires something beyond bifurcated ideologies. As the Second Vatican Council's, *Gaudium et spes*, describes, "the Church has always had the duty of scrutinizing the signs of the times and of interpreting them in the light of the Gospel" (GS, 4). But, this response in the light of Christ is not focused on the People of God alone. The Church gazes outwardly on the whole human race—regardless of nation, place, or religion—interacting with the world and living within it (GS, 40). Thus, the Church responds to the signs of the times by serving as a sign itself, promoting unity, human dignity, liberty, freedom, and the common good (GS, 27, 41–42).

The Church uniquely calls the faithful to this mission through the celebration of the Mass. In the Mass, in the unity of the Holy Spirit, we ask Christ to intercede for us to make things right—to take away our sins and to grant us mercy and peace. Certainly, requests for "mercy" or "peace" may not sound like calls for the world's transformation (GS, 38). But, God thinks differently. We may be asking for mercy and peace—but, for Jesus, bringing mercy and peace means setting the earth on fire (Luke 12:49–53; see *Go and Make Disciples*, 1–3).

If Jesus has come to set the earth ablaze, then our summons to "Go forth, the Mass is ended" (*Order of Mass*, 144) should feel more like jumping off a precipice than slipping out the back door after communion. Fire—especially the fire of the Holy Spirit—causes radical transformation. If we are seeking to become more closely bound with Christ Jesus, we are seeking not only to be transformed ourselves, but also to enter fully into Christ's mission to transform the world (GS, 38).

The following essay will explore the essential relationship of liturgy and the Church's response to the modern world by examining three different moments in twentieth- and twenty-first-century Catholicism: (1) the period of liturgical renewal in the twentieth century prior to the Council; (2) the Second Vatican Council itself; and (3) recent discussions surrounding the Eucharist and justice, including the work of the United States Council of Catholic Bishops and Pope Francis. Doing so will allow us to explore both historical and social developments regarding the intersection of liturgy and the modern world, particularly for American Catholicism, and key documents which develop their relationship.

Twentieth-Century Liturgical Renewal: Connecting Liturgy and Social Renewal

By the twentieth century, most lay faithful had become separated from the rituals and texts of the Mass itself, and had instead focused their spirituality in personal prayer, a myriad of important devotional exercises, and meditation on the Eucharist. Such worship was easily accessible, commonly known, and socially based. At the same time, devotional worship often expressed boundaries, and particular expressions were frequently colored by ethnic, social, or gendered divisions. The faithful's experience of worship, particularly when conducted during liturgical rites such as Mass, tended to accentuate the individual's role in the spiritual journey—completely unique from, and not particularly connected to, the neighbor sitting across the aisle in the pew, let alone the neighbor across the street, or across the globe.

With this rich yet splintered devotional world of Catholicism, advocates of liturgical renewal, beginning in the US context in the first quarter of the twentieth century, proposed something radically different. They proposed that, as one Church, the faithful were called to one, common expression of worship. They asked Catholics to refocus on the Mass itself and, furthermore, upon active and intelligent participation within this Mass. The faithful were invited to look to the Mass itself as their spiritual resource, and to come to know themselves not as individuals praying together, but as a social body, an integrated Body of Christ. Advocates of such initiatives were collectively referred to as members of the "liturgical movement."

This new vision of liturgy responded to invitations from twentieth-century popes, beginning, most notably, with Pope Pius X's *motu proprio* "On Sacred Music" of 1903. While this document focused on the importance of church music, it also expressed a fundamental key for understanding participation in the liturgy as important for living the Christian life and developing a "Christian spirit." Pius X described the faithful as "acquiring this spirit from its foremost and indispensable font, which is the active participation in the most holy mysteries and in the public and solemn prayer of the Church."[1]

But, this true Christian spirit was not only for the benefit of the faithful in the pews. In Pope Pius XI's encyclical on labor, *Quadragesimo Anno* (1931), he emphasized that in order to experience a restoration of "society according to the mind of the Church on the firmly established basis of social justice and social charity," there needed to be a "renewal of the Christian spirit" (QA, 126–127). Liturgical movement advocate Virgil Michel, OSB, quickly saw the connection between social justice and the liturgy:

> Pius X tells that the liturgy is the indispensable source of the true Christian spirit; Pius XI says that the true Christian spirit is indispensable for social regeneration. Hence the conclusion: The liturgy is the indispensable basis of Christian social regeneration.[2]

Such language clearly anticipated the Second Vatican Council's approach to both liturgy and the Church's role in the world. *Sacrosanctum concilium* would draw upon the image of the liturgy as a "source" and "font" for the Christian life, while documents such as *Gaudium et spes* would stress the Church's integral role in promoting social transformation.

Before any post-conciliar liturgical reforms occurred, the liturgical movement invited the faithful to both a physical remapping of the experience of liturgy as well as a spiritual reorientation. Regarding embodied, physical experience, the faithful were called

---

1. Pope Pius X, *On Sacred Music* (*Tra le Sollecitudini*) 22 November 1903.

2. Virgil Michel, "The Liturgy the Basis of Social Regeneration," *Orate Fratres* 9, no. 12 (1935): 545.

together to "practice" being the Body of Christ by acting as one body expressing its identity through the liturgy. This meant praying together, responding together, conducting postures and gestures together, and singing together.

With respect to spirituality, Mass was not simply an exercise to complete, but a forum for formation as the Body of Christ. Thus, liturgical movement advocates encouraged the faithful to set prayer cards and rosaries aside, and instead be shaped and informed by lectionary readings, the cycle of prayers in the missal, liturgical music and art, and the contours of the liturgical year.

Importantly, coming to know Christ through the experience of the Mass had significant implications for one's identity as a Christian. The preferred image of the liturgical movement was that of the Pauline-inspired "Mystical Body of Christ." Drawing on this motif, liturgical renewal advocates explained that, if liturgical worship formed one into the Body of Christ, then liturgical worship served as a rehearsal for how the faithful might respond to social crises, to economic disparity, to racial injustices, and to the need to care for and serve the poor. Thus, participation in the Mass both confirmed Christian identity and commissioned Christians to embrace their social responsibility to protect and support the marginalized and oppressed.

For example, Dorothy Day, cofounder of the *Catholic Worker* newspaper and organization, explained how the image of the Mystical Body of Christ inspired both social justice and liturgical renewal. Describing a day in the New York Catholic Worker house, she explained:

> Nearly all our friends who are interested in social justice from a Catholic point of view, from the very beginning of the paper [*The Catholic Worker*], have been equally interested in the Liturgical Movement [. . .]. But by now we are well accustomed to having most of the all-day discussions in our office come around eventually to the doctrine of the Mystical Body of Christ.[3]

3. The Editors, "From The Catholic Worker," *Orate Fratres* 8, no. 6 (1934): 284.

For Day, the Mystical Body of Christ image emphasized how each member of the Church had a responsibility to work for and love the other, a dynamic understanding of Church that responded to the acute needs of the Depression-era United States.

Nearly two decades later, Catholics continued to find inspiration in the Mass to overcome seemingly impossible American social problems. For example, describing her 1950s parish in Detroit, Michigan, parishioner Marriette Wickes explained:

> [T]he liturgy has been the source of building a unity between colored and white people. The fact that colored and white members of the choir sing the Mass together has flown over into community life outside the church. We have also built our parish social activities around the liturgy. For instance, for the last three years after the Easter Vigil there has been a breakfast in honor of the newly baptized with both colored and white preparing the meal, celebrating, congratulating and receiving the newly baptized into our parish family.[4]

Wickes' parish found that the liturgy allowed the faithful to push past the "color line" nearly a decade before significant Civil Rights legislation occurred in the United States.

Liturgical renewal advocates, such as Michel, Day, or Wickes, to name a few, affirmed, taught, and modeled how liturgical worship not only could but necessarily demanded that the faithful respond to social crises of their day—social crises that still mar the landscape of our contemporary world.

The Second Vatican Council: The Church's Role in the Modern World

The understanding of liturgy underwent a transformation over the course of the twentieth century that shaped how the Council described the liturgy, moving from an emphasis upon the importance of the transcendent and unchanging properties of the ritual,

---

4. Mariette Wickes, "Discussion," *1956 North American Liturgical Week Proceedings: People's Participation and Holy Week* (Elsberry, MO: The Liturgical Conference, 1957): 25–26.

to how the liturgy intersected with the needs of the times, pastoral situations, or even culture.

This shift in interpreting liturgy, which emphasized the significance of embodiment, history, and social realities, grew out of larger trends in the twentieth-century Catholic intellectual tradition. It also had important implications for how the Church even defined itself during the Council. The Council reframed the Catholic understanding of the Church from one that stood as a "Church militant" to a Church which stood as a "sign" and even a "sacrament" of Christ (e.g., LG, 1, 9, 48; GS, 42, 45; SC, 5, 26).

In turn, moving to an understanding of Church as "sign" impacted an understanding of how the Church and its worship might bring about social transformation for the People of God. Following the Council, the Church no longer assumed that "social transformation" meant that it would convert the world to Christ. Rather, if the Church served as a sign of the coming Kingdom of God, it would be the Church's responsibility to show forth to the world the authentic unity and peace, which characterized God's Kingdom. It was the Church's responsibility to admonish humanity to overcome strife, to support human associations that promoted justice, and to partner with the poor and afflicted (GS, 42). As *Gaudium et spes* poignantly begins, "The joys and the hopes, the grief and anguish of the people of our time, especially of those who are poor or afflicted, are the joys and hopes, the grief and anguish of the followers of Christ as well" (GS, 1).

Importantly, the summit and font for this Christian life was found in the liturgy, and especially the Eucharist. As *Lumen gentium* describes, "[I]n the sacrament of the Eucharistic bread, the unity of believers, who form one body in Christ, is both expressed and achieved" (LG, 3).[5] In short, the unity, which the Church invited the world to witness, was first realized in the eucharistic experience of the faithful. Therefore, the celebration of the Eucharist necessarily celebrated the People of God's mission to respond to the joys and hopes, the grief and anguish of the world, especially those of the poor and afflicted.

---

5. See Michael J. Tkacik, "Eucharist and Liturgy as Means to Social Justice in Vatican II," *Social Justice Review* 92, no. 5/6 (2001): 88–91.

And yet, in the years following the Council, the implicit connection between liturgy and justice has not been as clear as either liturgical movement advocates or Council members likely had hoped. The revision of liturgical rites that occurred following the Council absorbed an immense amount of energy, as the faithful received changes in language, ritual structure, and forms of art, music, or architecture, which were considered worthy of conveying the sacred. These "changes" were intended to execute the norms of *Sacrosanctum concilium*, such as the pastoral and teaching character of the liturgy (SC, 36), or the importance of inculturation (SC, 37). And, such issues certainly prompt pastoral concerns worthy of discussion and sensitivity. Yet, Roman Catholic time and attention regarding the Mass and the Eucharist have frequently remained focused on more superficial issues or aesthetical preferences, rather than on a consideration of the true aims of the Eucharist, which these changes were meant to facilitate.

After the Council: Connecting Liturgy and Justice

Nonetheless, in the years following the Council, the connection of liturgy and justice has emerged repeatedly, and worship has been affirmed as a source for social, political, and economic healing.

First, the USCCB's important pastoral letter on Catholic social teaching and the US economy, *Economic Justice for All* (1986), clearly affirmed the essential connection between Eucharistic inspiration and social action. As the document states:

> Worship and common prayer are the wellsprings that give life to any reflection on economic problems and that continually call the participants to greater fidelity to discipleship. To worship and pray to the God of the universe is to acknowledge that the healing love of God extends to all persons and to every part of existence, including work, leisure, money, economic and political power and their use, and to all those practical policies that either lead to justice or impede it. Therefore, when Christians come together in prayer, they make a commitment to carry God's love into all these areas of life. (EJA, 329)

Likewise, the liturgy has a significant role in teaching and transforming us from "self-seeking" persons looking for spirituality into disciples. The liturgy unites us in prayer with the whole people of God—rich and poor, in our neighborhoods and across our borders. And, the liturgy challenges us, asking us to question our ways of being and our values, and whether we are living in such a way that we are truly being a "visible sign of that unity in justice and peace that God wills for the whole of humanity" (EJA, 331).[6]

This understanding of the Eucharist leans heavily on the notion of discipleship—an important motif upon which both the US bishops and, more recently, Pope Francis have focused. Beginning in 1992, the US bishops issued *Go and Make Disciples,* which describes a hope to "foster gospel values in our society, promoting the dignity of the human person, the importance of the family, and the common good of oursociety" (GMD, 56). Worship that calls us to communion with our brothers and sisters inspires such discipleship (cf. GMD, 49).[7]

And yet, at times, amidst bishops' conversations regarding the Eucharist, focus has been placed upon forms of pastoral practice rather than pastoral implication. For example, at the October 2005 Synod, "The Eucharist: Source and Summit of the Life and Mission of the Church," some bishops chiefly expressed concerns about the correct observation of liturgical norms.[8] Others took issue with Eucharistic practices common after the Council, such as the move of the tabernacle to a Blessed Sacrament Chapel, or the distribution of communion in the palm.[9]

In contrast, at this same Synod, some bishops raised significant social and pastoral issues with respect to the Eucharist, such as Bishop Lucius Iwejuru Ugorji of Umuahia, Nigeria:

> If the eucharist brings about fraternal unity in the body of Christ, then the ever widening gap between the affluent and

---

6. United States Council of Catholic Bishops, *Economic Justice for All: Pastoral Letter on Catholic Social Teaching and the U.S. Economy* (November 1986), http://www.usccb.org/upload/economic_justice_for_all.pdf.

7. *Go and Make Disciples: A National Plan and Strategy for Catholic Evangelization in the United States* is an important resource for all ministers of the Church. The full text is found at http://www.usccb.org/beliefs-and-teachings/how-we-teach/evangelization/go-and-make-disciples/go-and-make-disciples-a-national-plan-and-strategy-for-catholic-evangelization-in-the-united-states.cfm.

8. "The Synod: A Multi-national Gathering," *Origins* 35, no. 19 (20 October 2005): 316–317.

9. "The Synod: A Multi-national Gathering," 317.

> the millions of poor people living in hunger and underserved misery in today's society is a great scandal (cf. 1 Corinthians 11:17–22). If Christians partake of the broken bread and the Lord's altar, they must be ready to work for a better and more just world for all. They must be prepared to be broken bread and to share bread with broken humanity.[10]

Likewise, an understanding of the Eucharist's implications for justice was reflected, more recently, on November 10, 2018, as Pope Francis addressed participants in the Plenary Assembly of the Pontifical Committee for International Eucharistic Congresses. Pope Francis asked how one could expect the Eucharist to have any impact in a world in which such intense forms of suffering exist:

> We think of families in difficulty, young people and adults without work, the sick and the elderly who are abandoned, migrants experiencing hardship and acts of violence—and rejected, and also many other forms of poverty.[11]

Yet, Francis argued that the Eucharist inspired a response to precisely such states of angst and apathy, explaining, "The celebration of the Eucharist thus becomes a cradle of attitudes that generate a Eucharistic culture, for it impels us to express in our way of life and our thinking the grace of Christ who gave of himself to the full."

For Pope Francis, such "Eucharistic attitudes" emphasize three major themes. First, "communion" with Christ and with one another demands that we "live in him and with him in charity and mission." Second, the Eucharist inspires us to service. By sharing in the Eucharistic liturgy, Christians adopt the fundamental command of John 13, where Jesus bends to wash the feet of his disciples and instructs them: "I have given you a model to follow, so that as I have done for you, you should also do" (John 13:15). Finally, Pope Francis describes the third of these "Eucharistic attitudes" as an attitude of mercy. Mercy has been a keyword of his pontificate, and he describes the Eucharist's power in making this mercy present to the world:

---

10. "The Synod," 323. See also David N. Power, "Eucharistic Justice," *Theological Studies* 67 (2006): 856–879.

11. Pope Francis, "Address of His Holiness Pope Francis to Participants in the Plenary Assembly of the Pontifical Committee for International Eucharistic Congresses," 10 November 2018, http://w2.vatican.va/content/francesco/en/speeches/2018/november/documents/papa-francesco_20181110_congressi-eucaristici.html.

> Everyone laments the corrosive river of misery flowing through our society. It is made up of different kinds of fear, oppression, arrogance, cruelty, hatred, forms of rejection and lack of concern for the environment, not to mention others. And yet, Christians realize every Sunday that this swollen river is powerless against the ocean of mercy that inundates our world. The Eucharist is the wellspring of this ocean of mercy, for in it the Lamb of God, slain yet standing, makes flow from his pierced side streams of living water. . . . Mercy thus enters the veins of this world and helps to form the image and structure of the People of God suited to our modern age.[12]

As Pope Francis teaches, the Eucharist demands that the faithful Body of Christ be oriented to communion with the human community, service to the poor and marginalized, and mercy in a world seemingly ignorant of it.

Conclusion

Understanding the Eucharist along lines of communion, service, and mercy flows from a long tradition of Eucharistic celebration and theology. Yet, in practical and pastoral circumstances, concerns about the Eucharist have tended not to explore these lines, but to focus on concerns less close to the heart of the Gospel. It may be difficult to recall the true end of Eucharist, when we can easily be caught up in the "nitty-gritty": the flow of the Eucharistic distribution and where the extraordinary ministers should stand, the ceremonial hand sanitizing for ministers of the Eucharist, whether the Precious Blood is distributed to the faithful, or even if that cup should leave the hands of the one administering it. Aside from this, concerns about the faithful's understanding of central questions of the Eucharist—such as real presence and transubstantiation—seem to plague the Church, and to inspire some of the concerned responses of Church leaders today.[13]

---

12. Ibid.

13. Gregory A. Smith, "Just One-Third of Catholics Agree with their Church that Eucharist is Body, Blood of Christ," Pew Research Center, 5 August 2019, https://www.pewresearch.org/fact-tank/2019/08/05/transubstantiation-eucharist-u-s-catholics/.

Nonetheless, the Church's firm desire to respond to the "needs of our own times" and the "world of today" resounds in the liturgy, and in places beyond the scope of petitions or announcements. The relationship between liturgy and the modern world is knit into the very words of our Eucharistic praying. As Eucharistic Prayer for Use in Masses for Various Needs III states:

> Grant that all the faithful of the Church,
> looking into the signs of the times by the light of faith,
> may constantly devote themselves
> to the service of the Gospel.
> Keep us attentive to the needs of all
> that, sharing their grief and pain
> their joy and hope,
> we may faithfully bring them the good news of salvation
> and go forward with them along the way of your Kingdom.
> (*The Roman Missal*, EPVNIII no. 7)

For us, today, when we hear the word "liturgy," neither lay nor clergy should become immediately distracted by our preferred style of vestments, liturgical translation, or musical genre. When we think of liturgy, we must remember we are celebrating our participation in Christ's mission, and accepting our own commission to go forth as disciples in a world deeply in need of a sign of God's Kingdom.

Questions for Discussion:

1. Consider the prayers, ritual actions, and readings of a recent Sunday celebration of the Mass. In what ways could this recent celebration of the Mass point us to Christian mission in our communities and wider world?
2. Why do we find connecting liturgy and justice challenging in our contemporary liturgical celebrations? What are possible ways these challenges could be overcome?
3. How can liturgically-inspired practices, such as the Rosary, Stations of the Cross or Eucharistic Adoration, inspire us to respond to social, economic, racial, ideological, and political disputes in the contemporary world?

3 Go and Make Disciples

MARK E. WEDIG, OP

As Roman Catholic Christians, we are constantly being evangelized by the Church's liturgy. We believe that our participation in the rituals of the Church open us to the workings of the Holy Spirit and deepen our conversion to Christ. We also know that the same liturgy that continually evangelizes us also will draw others to a deeper life in Christ through our genuine participation in these mysteries. Therefore, we believe that the Church's liturgy, especially when the Word of God is preached with joy and purpose and the liturgical rites reflect tremendous beauty and reverence, will embody the living presence of Christ for those who seek him. *Sacrosanctum concilium* (SC), reminds us of this evangelizing factor:

> While the liturgy daily builds up those who are within into a holy temple of the Lord, into a dwelling place for God in the Spirit, to the mature measure of the fullness of Christ, at the same time it marvelously strengthens their power to preach Christ, and thus shows forth the Church to those who are outside as a sign lifted up among the nations under which the scattered children of God may be gathered together, until there is one sheepfold and one shepherd. (2)

This constitution stresses that the liturgy is a principal dimension of evangelization.

In this essay I will explore how the liturgy fulfills the Church's mission to evangelize through four modalities, namely (a) the fundamental role of preaching in the liturgy, (b) the worshiping assembly as the locus of welcome, (c) the process of Christian initiation as a prime evangelizer, and (d) the dismissal rites in the liturgies of the Church as the commission to go and make disciples of those we meet in life's journey. Each of these means carries the Good News of Jesus Christ and transform people both inside and outside the fold.

Preaching in the Context of the Liturgy and Sacraments

Central to all aspects of Christian evangelization is the proclamation of the Word of God. In *Evangelii nuntiandi* (1975), Pope Paul VI addresses the imperative of preaching as fundamental to this mission of the Church. The pope emphasizes that preaching bridges the Gospel to the culture:

> The split between the Gospel and culture is without a doubt the drama of our time, just as it was of other times. Therefore, every effort must be made to ensure a full evangelization of culture, or more correctly of cultures. They have to be regenerated by an encounter with the Gospel. But this encounter will not take place if the Gospel is not proclaimed. (EN, 20)

Therefore, preaching encompasses all the ways that the Gospel is interpreted and deciphered for people who live in a specific time and place.

For the majority of Catholics, our encounter with the Word of God has been through the renewed and expanded service of Word in the sacramental celebrations of the post–Vatican II rites. Baptism, Eucharist, Penance, Anointing, Marriage, death and burial and other aspects of sacramental worship all open the Scriptures through a Liturgy of the Word affording the assembly the occasion to reflect deeply on how God's revelation speaks to various components of Christian life experience. In this context, the power of preaching in the form of the homily plays a unique role in Christian conversion. Pope Paul VI also reminds us of how the homily embodies that function:

> But at a time when the liturgy renewed by the Council has given greatly increased value to the Liturgy of the Word, it would be a mistake not to see in the homily an important and very adaptable instrument of evangelization. . . . The homily has a place and must not be neglected in the celebration of all the sacraments. . . . It will always be a privileged occasion for communicating the Word of the Lord. (EN, 43)

Therefore, preaching expressed through homiletic reflection remains a central vehicle for evangelization.

Nevertheless, the homily, although central to the preaching mission of the Church, does not encompass the whole scope of ecclesial proclamation. The vocation of preaching extends to all the baptized in their being anointed priest, prophet, and king (see *Evangelii gaudium*, 111–114). This vocation to preach especially includes the catechetical dimension of the proclaimed Word. Too often, the laity have not been formed to realize their call to preach to men and women who hunger for the Word in our world through personal faith witness and testimony at spiritual gatherings, in religious education, or ministries in healthcare, and so many aspects of Church life. These ministries take on an expressed liturgical dimension as they interface with the rites/process of Christian initiation, liturgies for children, hospital visitation, retreats, and other occasions for ritualized preaching.

Finally, both homiletic and other forms of preaching require a love for theology in order to bridge the Gospel and culture. The clergy and all the baptized who are privileged to preach formally in the context of the Church's liturgy carry the critical responsibility to study the signs of the times so as to carefully consider how to relate, explain, and elucidate the Christian tradition for others. Without a passion for theological reflection with an ear to the hearts of the people, preaching will always fall flat and fail to bridge Gospel and culture.

The worshipping assembly as locus of welcome

Many of us have heard the stories of those who have become alienated from the Christian assembly because they have experienced the

Church as unwelcoming and inhospitable. Evangelization hinges on the gathered Christian assembly serving as bridge and not barrier to hospitality. The US bishops in their national plan and strategy for evangelization, *Go and Make Disciples* (GMD), underline how our assemblies not only welcome those already at the center of the Church, but also invite those who have migrated to its fringes back to its center:

> We want to let our inactive brothers and sisters know that they always have a place in the Church and that we are hurt by their absence—as they are. We want to show our regret for any misunderstandings or mistreatment. And we want . . . to talk with them, share with them, and accept them as brothers and sisters. Every Catholic can be a minister of welcome, reconciliation, and understanding to those who have stopped practicing the faith. (40)

The success of Christian evangelization rests on overt gestures of inclusion that arise from the genuine desire to reach out to those estranged.

In *Evangelii gaudium* (EG), Pope Francis underscores that the welcome that evangelizes arises from a true and genuine joy. That authentic human encounter with Christ results in the experience of friendship with God, liberating us from narrowness and self-absorption. Some who express the most genuine joy ironically are heavily burdened by difficult circumstances of life. Yet their hearts have found joy in encounter with the risen Lord. Francis explains:

> I realize of course that joy is not expressed the same way at all times in life, especially at moments of great difficulty. Joy adapts and changes, but it always endures, even as a flicker of light born of our personal certainty that, when everything is said and done, we are infinitely loved. (6)

The evangelizing center of the Church welcomes others with a largesse resultant from an encounter with the joy of the Gospel.

The liturgy of the Church is authentic encounter of the risen Christ, which exudes that same joy. We are reminded that liturgy is a place of meeting up with God and not simply duty or obligation. Joyless liturgies are the antithesis of welcoming encounter, the antithesis of evangelization. How do our houses of prayer embody the joy of the Gospel characterized by Pope Francis? The renewal of the liturgy brought about in Vatican II emphasized that an encounter of the risen Christ is brought about through full, conscious, and active participation in the liturgical life of the Church. *Sacrosanctum concilium* states:

> The Church earnestly desires that all the faithful be led to that full, conscious, and active participation in liturgical celebrations called for by the very nature of the liturgy. Such participation by the Christian people as "a chosen race, a royal priesthood, a holy nation, God's own people," (1 Pt 2:9; see 2:4–5) is their right and duty by reason of their baptism.
>
> In the reform and promotion of the liturgy, this full and active participation by all the people is the aim to be considered before all else. For it is the primary and indispensable source from which the faithful are to derive the true Christian spirit. (14)

It is that genuine Christian spirit of participation that ultimately embodies the Christian welcome in the Church's liturgical life.

Christian hospitality embodied in the Church's liturgical expression not only welcomes people outside the fold into the assembly, but also receives the risen Christ who often comes to us as a stranger or alien. The Word of God must find hospitality through openness and the making of plenty good room,[1] especially in hearing the Word spoken. That form of hospitality arises from an interior disposition and receptivity to the Holy Spirit that is manifest through prayer and spiritual discipline.

Pope Francis exhorts the Church to be a place where mercy abounds and the Gospel is preached in word and deed. That temple of compassion and benevolence houses the external and internal manifestations of hospitality as exhorted by the pope in these words:

> The Church must be a place of mercy freely given, where everyone can feel welcomed, loved, forgiven and encouraged to live the good life of the Gospel. (EG, 114)

---

1. Cf. John 14:2; *Plenty Good Room* is an African American spiritual about the inclusiveness of God.

The *Rite of Christian Initiation of Adults* as Prime Evangelizer

Paragraphs 64–66 of *Sacrosanctum concilium* affirm that an adult catechumenate was to be restored in the life of the Catholic Church. In the years following Vatican II, work was done to restore a series of liturgical rites that would take place within a community of the faithful and would lead adults through a gradual process of evangelization and initiation. The process was conceived to span over several years, ranging from inquiry to eventual full initiation in the context of the Easter Vigil and then through a period of postbaptismal mystagogy. Thus, the *Rite of Christian Initiation of Adults* (RCIA) was born into the life of the Church.

The whole RCIA involves a comprehensive conception of evangelization directed to engage the entire community of believers with those inquiring in a process of deepening everyone's calling into the mystery of God's love. Therefore, the RCIA can be understood as prime evangelizer for both those already baptized and those inquiring, who collectively are converted to Jesus Christ by entering this process together. Unique to the RCIA is precisely its liturgical significance as evangelization practice. All levels of spiritual and religious transformation occur in the context of public, communal, ecclesial worship. In other words, all levels of conversion are publicly ritualized.

The whole RCIA can be understood as to what the Church is in relationship to its evangelizing function. The whole Church undergoes conversion together through the process of precatechumenate, catechumenate, election, initiation, and postbaptismal instruction. Catechesis is understood here as a broad methodology for transformation of the whole Church through a cycle of worship events. Consequently, the RCIA was designed not only for individual converts, but also for the ongoing conversion of the entire ecclesial community. Aidan Kavanagh captures that ecclesial significance by saying:

> The importance of the restored rites of adult initiation lies therefore less in its ceremonial details than in its strategic vision of the Church local and universal. It is a practical vision of what the Church is and can become through the

continuing renewal process of evangelization, conversion, catechesis, and the paschal sacraments of Christian initiation.[2]

The RCIA therefore broadens the concept of conversion to include the whole Church on the journey of religious transformation.

Nevertheless, the RCIA's Period of Evangelization and Precatechumenate does first stress the importance of identifying a stage of growing in deep sympathy to the Christian faith while remaining outside the Church's fold and therefore outside its liturgy per se. Yet even this stage of the RCIA identifies the helpfulness of ritualizing the inquiry of those standing at the door of the Church. The rite states:

> [I]f circumstances suggest and in keeping with local custom, [the conference of bishops may provide] a preliminary manner of receiving those interested in the precatechumenate, that is, those inquirers who, even though they do not fully believe, show some leaning toward the Christian faith (and who may be called "sympathizers"). (39)

The RCIA stresses that any preliminary ritualizing of an incipient faith must adapt itself uniquely to the local culture at large.

As the inquirer moves from "sympathizer" to more articulated *conversus* to the Christian faith, the first rituals of the prebaptized in the RCIA warrant what it means to overcome the evil that weighs down the human condition and live in the presence of the Holy Spirit. Through the liturgical structures of exorcism and scrutiny, the Church attempts to find the language of how to grapple with deliverance from forces that separate us from God. Rita Ferrone addresses that liberation from the bonds of evil in the life of the prebaptized:

> Modern people may doubt the existence of evil spirits and feel awkward about addressing them as personal figures, but they don't doubt the existence of evil or the need to pray for deliverance.[3]

---

2. Aidan Kavanagh, *The Shape of Baptism: The Rite of Christian Initiation* (Collegeville, MN: Liturgical Press, 1978), 127.

3. Rita Ferrone, "Scrutiny, Exorcism, and the Construction of the Christian Self," *Catechumenate* 33 no. 1 (January 2011): 20.

Adults who seek Baptism also seek release from death-dealing factors, which often have ensnared persons in environments of evil. The RCIA becomes a primary way that liberation from evil finds expression in the lives of both those to be initiated and those who accompany them. The ritual of exorcism in the Rite of Acceptance into the Order of Catechumens and the minor exorcisms that follow during the Period of the Catechumenate embody that liberation. Roger Béraudy explains:

> The function of exorcism is to "conjure" and expel the presence of that other-than-myself, to whom I yield whenever I sin, and who is the adversary of him who saves me.[4]

It is the work of the liturgy to name and stand against these forces.

The RCIA maps a journey of the prebaptized through carefully constructed ritual events that correspond to stages of conversion in the life of the *conversi,* but also in the life of all who grow continuously in the Christian life, especially those who accompany the *conversi*. The journey of the inquirer or sympathizer is distinct from the catechumen who is different from the elect who becomes fully initiated. The road from one to the next of these stages of conversion is punctuated by a more articulated intentionality of the faith. Each stage crescendos into the next. This progressively intensifying transformation takes place ritually in the midst of the assembly. Therefore, the RCIA is a prime evangelizer because it simultaneously deepens the transformation of those fully initiated and those along the way through its orchestrated liturgy.

The entire RCIA mirrors the life of the paschal journey of the Christian life. Its orchestration of ritual follows the movement of passion, death, and Resurrection as it is understood in the life of Christian conversion. The rite instructs:

> The whole initiation must bear a markedly paschal character, since the initiation of Christians is the first sacramental sharing in Christ's dying and rising and since, in addition, the period of purification and enlightenment ordinarily coincides with Lent and the period of

4. Roger Béraudy, SS, "Scrutinies and Exorcisms," in *Adult Baptism and the Catechumenate*, ed. Johannes Wagner, *Concilium*, vol. 22 (New York: Paulist Press, 1967), 61.

postbaptismal catechesis of mystagogy with the Easter season. (RCIA, 8)

That paschal character will find its greatest ritual expression in the Easter Vigil where the elect become neophytes and where the entire assembly reenters its paschal journey with them and is, once again, transformed by their liturgical participation year after year.

The Dismissal Rites as the Great Commission to Make Disciples of Our Brothers and Sisters on the Way

It might at first seem trivial to consider the Dismissal Rites that conclude the liturgies of the Church as integral to a theology of liturgical evangelization. Yet, as suggested here, one might ponder how in a variety of liturgical settings, going forth to serve the Lord embodies a much larger reality of what it means to take leave from the liturgy as a commissioned disciple. Susan Roll in her commentary on the Dismissal Rite of the Order of the Mass explains this fuller significance:

> In spite of their relative brevity and their starkly functional character, the concluding rites conceal a rich variety of associations with the nature of what it means to live one's Christian faith outside the walls of the church building. The operative theology of these rites involves nothing less than the commission given in baptism to all Christians to live and preach the Good News in every aspect of their lives.[5]

This commission is no small measure of what it means to truly take what is gained in liturgy to the world around us.

Therefore, in this last section on liturgy and mission, it would profit us to examine what it means to go forth from the various rites of the Church to serve and love as an agent of evangelization. As Roll suggests above, the commission given in Baptism to live and preach the Gospel remains the fundamental commission for

---

5. Susan Roll, "The Concluding Rites: Theology of the Latin Text and Rite," *A Commentary on the Order of the Mass of The Roman Missal*, ed. Edward Foley (Collegeville, MN: Liturgical Press, 2011), 635.

intentional discipleship for every Christian. How liturgical participation readies us for the evangelizing task is key to this consideration. In other words, how does a deliberate and purposeful liturgical life prepare us for the task of making disciples of others?

The real question raised here about the liturgical dismissal rites focuses on what is the ultimate relationship between liturgy and life; that the true function of worship is to give Christians a practical knowledge of the abiding connection between their religious identity and their ordinary lives. Therefore, the liturgy is hardly just a distinct or unique religious ritual that revolves around itself; it is the point of transformation of each person, of humankind and of all creation by Christ, through the Spirit, to the glory of the Father. If the liturgy does not connect us to the way we live our lives then it remains simply a perfunctory and futile exercise. Said plainly, the rule of prayer mediates the rule of faith. Aidan Kavanagh conveys this as follows:

> [T]he liturgy of a church is nothing other than that church's faith in motion on certain and definite levels. . . . [A] church's worship does not merely reflect or express its repertoire of faith. It transacts the church's faith in God under the condition of God's real presence in both church and world. . . . Therefore the liturgy is not merely one ecclesiastical "work" or one theological datum among others. It is simply the church living its "bread and butter" life of faith under grace, a life in which God in Christ is encountered regularly and dependably as in no other way for the life of the world.[6]

This church/world relation is bridged by liturgical participation. Therefore, the liturgy is the great evangelizer in that our life witness grows out from it and then returns there. Intrinsic to liturgy is that Christian people embody with their life what has been symbolized in the sacramental and liturgical life of the local Church.

Yet, symmetries between liturgy and life are not easy connections to be made in the contemporary world. Often the harsh circumstances of the hyperreal and radically pluralistic world challenge such correlations. Religious claims are often subverted by increasingly

6. Aidan Kavanagh, *On Liturgical Theology* (Collegeville, MN: Liturgical Press, 1984), 8.

complicated and competitive social, economic, philosophical, and religious factors. If the liturgy remains a source for continued evangelization in the Church, it bears an ever-greater burden of adaptation, integration, and even resistance to complex postmodern factors.[7]

Liturgical evangelization requires engaging the world without simply succumbing to it. Therefore, authentic liturgical participation necessitates wise and discerning hearts that critically interpret the relationship between liturgy and life. What in the culture forces the Church to change and adapt its liturgical expression? What in the Church's liturgy, by its nature, resists cultural assimilation? Nevertheless, the evangelizing factor affirms that it is possible to identify and affirm the transformative potential precisely in the juxtaposition of daily life with the mysteries of God's presence despite cultural, social, and religious incongruities and challenges. A proper Christian evangelization through the liturgy is not characterized by a romantic and naive return to premodern ecclesial expressions, but by the rites adapted to contemporary place and time. Therefore, authentic liturgical inculturation is an essential function of Christian evangelization.

Finally, that critical response in liturgical participation rests in communities of the faithful who truly comprehend the meaning of their actions. Evangelization and critical understanding go hand in hand, welcoming the challenge of connecting liturgy and life. Pope John Paul II in his apostolic letter *Dies Domini* expresses that challenge of connecting the Sunday to daily life:

> For the faithful who have understood the meaning of what they have done, the eucharistic celebration does not stop at the church door. Like the first witnesses of the resurrection, Christians who gather each Sunday to experience and proclaim the presence of the Risen Lord are called to evangelize and bear witness in their daily lives. Given this, the prayer after communion and the concluding rite—the final blessing and the dismissal—need be better valued and appreciated, so that all who have shared in the eucharist may come to a deeper sense of the responsibility that is entrusted to them. Once the assembly disperses, Christ's

---

7. Mark E. Wedig, "Evangelization, Inculturation, and the RCIA," *Worship* 76, no. 6 (November 2002): 504.

> disciples return to their everyday surroundings with the commitment to make their whole life a gift, a spiritual sacrifice pleasing to God. (45)

Conclusion

In this essay, I investigated how the liturgy achieves the Church's mission to evangelize through four modalities, namely the fundamental role of preaching in the liturgy, the worshipping assembly as the locus of welcome, the RCIA as a prime evangelizer, and the dismissal rites in the liturgies of the Church as the commission to go and make disciples of those we meet in life's journey. Each of these manners of liturgical expression uniquely mediates the Church's proclamation of the Lord Jesus in the world around us, manifesting the risen Lord for the evangelization of the world.

Questions for Discussion:

1. Although the homily remains central to the preaching and evangelization mission of the Church, it does not encompass the whole scope of ecclesial proclamation. Discuss the ways in which the vocation of preaching is exercised by all the baptized through liturgical expression outside the context of the homily.
2. Evangelization hinges on the gathered assembly serving as a bridge to hospitality, especially welcoming the inactive brothers and sisters into the fold. Discuss how our houses of worship can embody the joy of the Gospel characterized by Pope Francis, making room for new members through hospitality.
3. The RCIA is identified as "prime evangelizer" both for those already baptized and those inquiring by participation in a common evangelization process together. Discuss how this corporate conversion is unique to the Periods of the Precatechumenate, the Catechumenate, and Mystagogy, as well as the stages of election and initiation.

4 Liturgical Catechesis and Mystagogy

CHRISTIAN McCONNELL

In any community familiar with the complexity and richness of liturgical worship, there will always be an attraction to having things explained. Eye-opening moments and cries of "*So that's* why we do that!" can help even long-time members of the community feel more enriched and engaged. It may be tempting to think that these conversations are what we mean by "liturgical catechesis."

With the requirement that sacraments can only be celebrated when those "receiving" the sacraments (or their parents) have been properly prepared, one might instinctively think that the main point of such preparation is to explain the sacraments themselves. The assumption is that no one can properly benefit from the grace of a sacrament without first understanding how to think about it. Alternatively, it is often tempting to approach sacramental preparation as an opportunity to catechize about everything else: the first or only celebration of any sacrament is seen as a window of opportunity to explain not only the sacraments, but also everything worth knowing.

However, catechesis *about* the liturgy, especially when reduced to explanation, is insufficient. It falls short of what liturgical catechesis really is. It can lead people to assume that the meaning of liturgical symbols can be expressed in tidy "correct answers" that summarize the symbol, and ultimately, render the symbol itself unnecessary. Once one knows the "correct answer," once the code has been cracked, there is nothing more to be found in the meaning of the symbol. If this kind of decoding is the approach to preparing for a sacrament, it can also lead to a sense that the celebration of the liturgy is the conclusion of a process of understanding rather than the beginning of one.

The nature of liturgical symbol calls for something more open-ended, which respects how rich and multivalent true symbols are. If an explanation is provided in advance for what the symbol means, then in the event itself other meanings may not be communicated; the "right answer" will push other possibilities out of mind. This leads many liturgists to insist that the liturgy should not be explained at all—that if it is celebrated well, it should be able to speak for itself. This is true to a point. On the other hand, no symbol means anything outside of a context of signification. If the liturgy is simply allowed to speak, without any commentary at any time, lack of context may lead the symbol to say nothing at all. Therefore, some kind of catechesis does need to accompany a life of entering into the liturgy, providing a fruitful soil for the liturgy to be planted and flourish.

In determining what the ideal relationship is between liturgy and catechesis, one needs to ask what the purpose of the catechesis really is. Why do we want to explain the liturgy in simplified ways? Often when liturgists speak about catechesis, they really mean explaining liturgical practices, telling everyone why we do them. Sometimes there is an ulterior motive: if we explain why we do things, the people in the pews will be cooperative and go along with what we are planning to do, especially if we are trying to make changes in the way we celebrate. However, this is not really catechesis at all. Faith formation includes an intellectual dimension, striving for greater cognitive understanding, but an entirely cognitive approach doesn't respect the way liturgy and faith itself speak to the whole person. The liturgy becomes an object of our explanations, instead of a "source and summit" that forms all of us, in the richness of our whole faith experience.

Rather than catechesis *about* the liturgy, liturgical catechesis and mystagogy will be described here in terms of two complementary movements between liturgy and life, grounded in essential principles of liturgical practice. The imperative of "full, conscious, and active participation" calls for catechesis *for* the liturgy, guiding people into the attitudes, practices, and values that one needs to have to be able to enter into that participation (*Sacrosanctum concilium*, 14). Recognizing the liturgy as the "source and summit" of the Christian life calls for catechesis *from* the liturgy, or mystagogy.[1] In this approach, liturgy is not so much explained as interpreted, opening up new understandings of faith itself, not just as believed, but also as lived.

It should be noted that sometimes the terms "liturgical catechesis" and "mystagogy" are used interchangeably. Here, however, they will be used to name these two complementary movements: (1) forming lived faith to make participation in the liturgy possible and (2) turning to liturgy to make growth in faith possible. These complementary movements are never separate; in well-formed faith, believers routinely and easily correlate their liturgical experience and their life experience, back and forth in creative ways. This distinction should not be pushed too far, as they are different sides of the same coin. But paying attention to both sides is valuable if catechesis is really going to be driven by what the liturgy really needs.

Catechesis *for* Liturgy: Liturgical Catechesis

One of the most important principles of liturgy is expressed in *Sacrosanctum concilium*:

> The Church earnestly desires that all the faithful be led to that full, conscious, and active participation in liturgical celebrations called for by the very nature of the liturgy. Such participation by the Christian people as 'a chosen race, a royal priesthood, a holy nation, God's own people' is their right and duty by reason of their baptism. (14)

It mentions further that pastors are to see to the "necessary instruction" to make this possible. At first, this might seem like simple coaching, so that everyone knows his or her lines, and knows when to sit, stand, and kneel down, but that kind of preparation only

1. In *Saying Amen: A Mystagogy of Sacrament*, Kathleen Hughes says, "*Mystagogy* is a word borrowed from Greek; it means, literally, the 'interpretation of mystery' or the 'teaching of mystery'" (9).

provides for participation that is "active." A great deal more is needed if the faithful's participation is to be fully conscious.

The *General Directory for Catechesis* (GDC) expands slightly on what that necessary instruction might be. It names "liturgical education" as one of the six tasks of catechesis. "Knowledge of the faith" is only one of the others. The rest are "moral formation," "teaching to pray," "education for community life," and "missionary initiation" (GDC, 85). It is easy to see how liturgy relates not only to the task of "liturgical education," but also to all six. While liturgy is an indispensable source for all of them, "liturgical education" is described as not just understanding the liturgy, but also being formed in such a way as to be able to participate in the liturgy in the first place:

> For this reason, catechesis, along with promoting a knowledge of the meaning of the liturgy and the sacraments, must also educate the disciples of Jesus Christ "for prayer, for thanksgiving, for repentance, for praying with confidence, for community spirit, for understanding correctly the meaning of the creeds . . . ," as all of this is necessary for a true liturgical life. (GDC, 85)

This demands attention when we undertake "sacramental preparation." Far from merely walking through the sacrament to be celebrated and taking care of logistics, liturgical catechesis needs to run much deeper. It includes cognitive understanding, but must also cultivate habits, attitudes, and values that need to be there if truly "conscious and active" liturgical participation can happen at all.

Devout, committed people of faith might think some of these habits and attitudes are intuitive or natural. We might assume that any human being can simply be invited to join in prayer, thanksgiving, repentance, or community spirit. But in an increasingly secularized and pluralistic world, we need to stop assuming that either children or adults can do these things easily, with a fully engaged heart. We assume some things are just automatic, when in reality they may not be.

Proper liturgical catechesis takes note of all of the attitudes that liturgical participation demands. Forming habits in the rest of life then can be brought to doing the liturgy. Several habits or attitudes, but by no means all, can be mentioned here. Fundamental to liturgical prayer is gratitude—acknowledgement of the blessings one experiences in life and attributing them to God's grace. Of course, liturgical prayer routinely moves from thanksgiving to petition. We need to have the habit of turning to God in our needs, and placing trust in God (and after all, trust is the real meaning of "faith.") The believer needs to learn to turn outward from oneself, acknowledging that the ultimate reality in life is God who is love. This should also lead to a habit of valuing and building relationships with others, not only as individuals, but in community. This could be a challenge in an individualistic culture.

We are in no position to attend "fully and consciously" to the Word of God in the liturgy, unless we have cultivated a spirituality of hearing the Word, learning to assume that through the Holy Spirit, the Word really does have something to say to each of us. As the Word of God in all its forms is highly intertextual, we also need a basic literacy in the fundamental narratives of the faith, the stories that define the faith community.

We cannot truly appreciate the celebration of sacraments without an underlying attitude of sacramentality, seeing creation (both nature and human experience) as good, and as imbued with God's grace. It is entirely possible to go through one's life without really recognizing grace; if we cannot recognize it in daily life, then we will fail to recognize it in sacramental worship. We need to be formed in a habit of listening for the call of God in our own lives and appreciating the fullness of our baptismal vocation. We should be open to the activity of the Holy Spirit, which drives us outward in mission in the world.

All of these are basic building blocks of a life of faith, but they are also essential for anyone to enter into full participation in the liturgy, not just "actively" but "consciously," and not just with the mind, but also with the heart. To be sure, the very best teacher of these habits and attitudes is the liturgy itself. The liturgy, after all, is "source and summit" of the whole Christian life. But in order to flourish, liturgical participation needs the support of this kind of catechesis, developing these habits outside of the liturgy as well. In all of this, there is an especially important place for the home; going all the way back to its Jewish roots, Christian worship has always had a place not only for the public sphere, but also for the domestic. The "source and summit" is not the "be all and end all." Liturgical catechesis for the liturgy can rely heavily on the role of parents as the primary educators in the faith, if those parents are themselves formed well in these habits and attitudes to begin with.

Liturgical catechesis needs to recognize that these habits and attitudes cannot simply be assumed. Many of us might not remember how we learned them, but we did somehow, and the same opportunity to learn them by "osmosis" may not exist anymore in a changing society. Parishes need to enable people to cultivate these habits in any way they can. Most importantly, these attitudes and habits show why mere explanation of the liturgy is completely inadequate.

Catechesis *from* Liturgy: Mystagogy

The concept of the liturgy as the "source and summit" also comes from *Sacrosanctum concilium*:

> The sacred liturgy does not exhaust the entire activity of the Church. . . . Nevertheless, the liturgy is the summit toward which the activity of the Church is directed; at the same time it is the font from which all her power flows. (9–10)

If liturgical catechesis is to form us in life to be able to celebrate the liturgy, it is even more essential that the "source and summit" continually shape the rest of our faith and practice. We need to be formed in the habit of finding deeper and deeper meaning in the liturgy and applying it to our understanding of the life of faith, allowing it to shape our behavior, attitudes, and fundamental values. This is the mystagogical dimension.

Mystagogy is more than simply the final stage of the RCIA. As with evangelization in the first stage, mystagogy should be not so much a phase in an RCIA process as a continuous part of the life of the Church. Just as the whole Church should be committed to evangelization, leading some into the process of the catechumenate, so too should the whole Church believe, pray, and grow with a mystagogical sensibility, in which neophytes continue long past the Easter season.

The basis of mystagogy is the same principle that gives rise to liturgical theology, the usual shorthand of which is *lex orandi, lex credendi*. In the classic definition of theology as "faith seeking understanding," that act of "seeking understanding" needs to turn to liturgy as one of its primary sources. So too, as believers attempt to grow in their faith, and seek to understand their own lives and experience, they need to develop the habit of looking to the liturgy to provide that meaning. This is why, in mystagogy, the experience of the liturgy comes first. The rites are not simply an expression of predetermined ideas (as is assumed when one just tries to "explain" the "right answer"). In this sort of movement between liturgy, faith, and life, the rites are there first, supplying an inexhaustible range of meaning.

In mystagogy, the experience of the rites is the source for preaching, catechesis, and personal reflection. In the fourth-century roots of the RCIA, this meant that catechesis on the rites of initiation themselves came after they were celebrated. In much the same way that adult learning theories emphasize today, sometimes there's no substitute for experiencing something first, to reflect upon it later, as described by Cyril of Jerusalem:

> For some time now, true and beloved children of the Church, I have desired to discourse to you on these spiritual and celestial mysteries. But I well knew that visual testimony is more trustworthy than mere hearsay, and therefore I awaited this chance of finding you more amenable to my words, so that out of your personal experience I could lead you into the brighter and more fragrant meadow of Paradise on earth. The moment is especially auspicious, since you became receptive to the more heavenly mysteries when you were accounted worthy of divine and vitalizing baptism.[2]

Despite its importance, the section on mystagogy in the RCIA is actually quite brief, describing it in only eight paragraphs. The period after the celebration of the initiation sacraments is called "a time for the community and the neophytes together to grow in deepening their grasp of the paschal mystery and in making it part of their lives through meditation on the Gospel, sharing in the eucharist, and doing the works of charity" (RCIA, 234). The newly baptized are "introduced into a fuller and more effective understanding of mysteries through the Gospel message they have learned and above

2. Cyril of Jerusalem, *Mystagogical Catecheses*, no. 1, in *The Awe-Inspiring Rites of Initiation: The Origins of the RCIA* (Collegeville, MN: Liturgical Press, 1994), 70.

all through their experience of the sacraments they have received" (RCIA, 235). They are also expected to grow in relationship with the community into which they have been initiated. They "should experience a full and joyful welcome into the community and enter into closer ties with the other faithful" (RCIA, 236).

The RCIA does not say much about how "the distinctive spirit and power of the period of postbaptismal catechesis or mystagogy derive from the new, personal experience of the sacraments and of the community" other than discussing the importance of Masses for the neophytes in the Easter season (RCIA, 247). This brevity about how mystagogy is to be done leaves its interpretation and application wide open, if catechists only consider what is said in the rite itself. In the worst cases, sometimes it is simply a continuation of "classes" after Easter. In better cases, there is more serious attention given to inviting the neophytes to reflect upon their experience of the sacraments, although sometimes the interpretation of the liturgy does not go much beyond "what did it seem to mean to you?"

If the rite itself is brief, it becomes even more valuable to look at the sources it was built upon. The homilies of the great mystagogues[3] of the early Church show a rich, creative set of strategies for finding depth of meaning in the experience of the rites. Sometimes, this even included an acknowledgement that the rites themselves did not communicate everything they could in the moment. As Tertullian noted in the third century:

> Because with such complete simplicity, without display, without any unusual equipment, and (not least) without anything to pay, a man is sent down into the water, is washed to the accompaniment of very few words, and comes up little or no cleaner than he was, his attainment to eternity is regarded as beyond belief.[4]

But as the word mystagogy implies, the whole point of mystagogical catechesis is to open up for those who have experienced the

---

3. In *Experience the Mystery: Pastoral Possibilities for Christian Mystagogy*, David Regan says, "The 'mystagogue' is the person who" leads the neophyte; the one "who introduces the candidate into the divine mysteries" (11).

4. Tertullian, *De Baptismo 2*, in Edward Charles Whitaker and Maxwell E. Johnson, *Documents of the Baptismal Liturgy* (Collegeville, MN: Liturgical Press, 2003), 9.

sacraments a depth that was not obvious in the experience itself. As Ambrose said:[5]

> You came into the baptistery, you saw the water, you saw the bishop, you saw the levite [priest]. And if anyone should perhaps be thinking of saying: 'Is that all?' I say, indeed it is all. There truly is all, where there is all innocence, all devotion, all grace, all sanctification. You saw all you could see with the eyes of the body, all that is open to human sight. You saw what is seen, but not what is done. What is unseen is much greater than what is seen: 'because the things that are seen are transient, but the things that are unseen are eternal.'[6]

This means that despite the importance of richly celebrated liturgy, with an evocative communication of meaning, there will always be more to be found in it. How is catechesis to undertake this task, without falling back into the trap of "explaining" the "correct answer"? The solution comes in the nature of symbol, which does not mean anything without a context. Mystagogy is the act of supplying the context, on many levels. It is helping those who experience the sacraments to draw connections: between liturgy and the important narratives of the faith in the Scriptures; between liturgy and the created world around us; between liturgy and human life in community. A mystagogue models this process and draws out these connections so we can all learn the habit of "reading" the liturgical symbols with new or renewed vision.

Michael Joncas' excellent treatment of how the interpretation is done, rich with many examples from patristic homilists themselves, summarizes their approach as relating the liturgical symbols to the cosmic symbolism of nature, human experience, scriptural narratives, and the prescription of Christian behavior.[7] When we think back to the waters of the font, we can recall the waters of creation, so that we are re-created in them; or the waters of the womb, from which we have been reborn; or the waters of the Red Sea,

---

5. For a rich and very practical study of Ambrose's approach, see *Craig Satterlee, Ambrose of Milan's Method of Mystagogical Preaching* (Collegeville, MN: Liturgical Press, 2002).

6. Yarnold, *The Awe-Inspiring Rites of Initiation*, 104.

7. See Michael Joncas, *Preaching the Rites of Christian Initiation*, Forum Essays, no. 4 (Chicago: Liturgy Training Publications, 1994), ch. 4.

so that we, too, must have been freed from some kind of slavery into a new kind of freedom. This correlation of liturgical symbols with Scripture and experience is a creative process, with very little limitation. It simply posits that if the sacraments are a participation in salvation history (and they are), then when the liturgical symbol is similar to elements of Scriptural narratives or human life, then God must be working the same way in us as in those other examples. Once the parallel is drawn, context is supplied, and the symbols speak more richly.

To be sure, this type of catechesis seems unfamiliar to us today, but it is very important that we practice learning to do it. It can be applied to the entire liturgy, not just the rites of initiation, and for all of us, not just for the newly baptized. When we partake of the cup at the Eucharist, for example, we should be able to relate it to the wine the prophets mention as a sign of the abundance of the "day of the Lord," fulfilled in the wine in Jesus' first sign, at Cana. We should be able to drink of that cup and be reminded of Jesus' question, "Can you drink the cup that I must drink?" (cf. Matthew 20:22). This is Jesus' challenge to share in his self-sacrifice and even his death.

These sorts of associations are not automatic. It is an important challenge for catechesis to embrace its mystagogical side, not just in the RCIA, but also in the life of the whole Church. We all need to be formed more and more in the habit of drawing these connections, first by having talented preachers and catechists model it for us, but also by having faith-sharing opportunities to practice doing it ourselves. This is a form of catechesis that is poetic, not didactic; it is inductive, not deductive, and it does not seek a "correct answer" that will put an end to our seeking.

Some Practical Considerations

So what are some practical implications we can learn and apply from these complementary approaches? Primarily, while there will always be a place for explanations about the liturgy, it is far more important to form people for their participation in the liturgy, and to undertake faith formation from what the liturgy offers us. The liturgy should not be an object of explanation, but a source of life.

We need to avoid assuming that the attitudes and habits the liturgy requires are somehow intuitively obvious to all those we serve. Accompanying all of God's people in their walk of faith, we should recognize that lived example speaks louder than words, modeling the lived experience the liturgy both assumes and reshapes. Liturgical catechesis should provide plenty of opportunities to reflect upon experience, interpret experience, and practice prayer and ritual.

When we do speak, we should speak in ways that are evocative, that invite people to deeper reflection, rather than trying to settle everything. We should draw connections between liturgical rites, Scriptural narratives, and real-life human experience. More than simply doing it for them, we need to invite the faithful to do so for themselves. Beyond simply asking, "What did it mean to you?" we should be supplying the narratives that define our faith, and ask instead, "How is this story your story, too?" The symbolic words and actions of the liturgy should be a path into a whole way of looking at the world, revealing God's gracious presence, rather than a code to be deciphered. This type of engagement truly leads us to a profound encounter with the paschal mystery. An exercise in trivia can be interesting, but it cannot inspire conversion.

Ultimately, as we all grow in the habit of seeing liturgy in light of life, and life in light of liturgy, we should all feel energized to live up to the identity the liturgy gives us, sharing our faith in mission. Our participation in the mission of Christ is the sign that our participation in the liturgy is truly bearing fruit.

Questions for Discussion:

1. How can the "domestic Church" help to form young people in the attitudes and habits that enable them to participate in the liturgy with full mind and heart? What sorts of practices nurture prayer and ritual?

2. How can a parish community find ways to invite people to reflect upon their experience of the liturgical rites, in a meaningful way? What opportunities are there for those who serve in liturgical ministries, as well as for those "in the pews"?
3. Instead of "explaining away" the liturgy, what might an open-ended approach to liturgical catechesis look like?

5 Lead Us Into the Light: A Primer on Liturgy and Social Justice

ERIC T. STYLES

Sing a song full of faith that the dark past has taught us,
Sing a song full of the hope that the present has brought us;
Facing the rising sun of our new day begun,
Let us march on till victory is won.[1]

I

Lyricist and poet James Weldon Johnson, along with his composer-brother John Rosamond Johnson, penned a hymn that captures the connections we will explore in this essay: the relationship between liturgy and social justice. We might ask, To where are they marching and what victory do they hope to win? Drawing from the tragic and triumphant history of the African American experience, the singers are marching on not as much to a place, but to a state of being where justice prevails. Yet, it is on the way to this "state," in the actual singing of this song, that a foretaste of God's fullness and truth can be received.

1. Johnson, James Weldon, and John Rosamond Johnson. "Lift Every Voice and Sing." *Lead Me, Guide Me: The African American Catholic Hymnal* (Chicago: GIA Publications, 1987), 291.

The challenge here is not a new one: What is the proper relationship between upright worship and righteous social action? How do contemplation and action inform one another? Can "churchy" people and "social justice" people find common ground? One American exemplar of living deeply embedded in a world where worship of God is fundamentally attentive to the Christian call to justice is the Rev. Dr. Martin Luther King Jr. In a passage well known as Dr. King's favorite, the prophet Amos warns the Israelites that worship and liturgy without a commitment to justice is more than empty; it is sacrilege:

> Take away from me the noise of your songs;
> I will not listen to the melody of your harps.
> But let justice roll down like waters,
> and righteousness like an ever-flowing stream.
> (Amos 5:23–24)

Now we turn to focus our attention on how members of the Body are formed as Christian disciples, how they live out social justice. In order to ground this reflection in concrete pastoral realities, let us imagine a few scenarios where the issue at hand might manifest itself today:

> The neighborhood your parish serves is changing; immigrants are moving in. Perhaps they speak a different language. Perhaps the subtle details of how they worship is shifting the common practice. Longstanding worshipers are beginning to feel less comfortable at the liturgy. What does the parish leadership do?

> There has been a good deal of gun violence in the community. Some of it is related to poverty, and some to distorted ideologies. Prayer services are often planned. Vigil after vigil is organized. What does it really matter?

> The Bishop writes a pastoral letter on racism and the pastor decides to preach on the topic for a few weeks. People find the experience off-putting. Shouldn't the liturgy be "apolitical"?

These are actual scenarios that happen in parishes across the country. Parishioners respond to them from the vantage point of their own personalities, upbringing, political dispositions, and liturgical tastes. What vantage point should inform the response of the parish as a whole? Should there be a perspective that shapes the community's responses?

The Judeo-Christian tradition is filled with resources and examples of (1) the relationship between worship and justice being consistently contentious; and (2) the prophetic traditions maintaining that they are inextricably linked. This reflection continues, first with an introductory treatment of the Christian concept of social justice. Second, we will lay out foundations for seeing the liturgy as space in which Christians are formed as individual selves and active members of a community. Third, we will explore how that formational experience is rooted in the work of justice preparing Christians to be incorporated directly into the Just One, ready and willing to live as he did. Lastly, we will return to some ongoing questions about the liturgy's effectiveness as justice formation and the liturgy's ability to be just in itself.

II

What is Justice?

Sixth-century Roman law as codified in the *Institutes of Justinian* described justice as "the constant and perpetual will to render each his due."[2] Justice has always been associated with fairness and moral rectitude: we give one another what we owe or what is owed. David Miller highlights four aspects embedded in this classic definition:

1. Justice is owed to persons, individually first and sometimes to groups of individuals.
2. Justice is owed, meaning we have a right to claim it, and sometimes even to demand it.

2. David Miller, "Justice," in *The Stanford Encyclopedia of Philosophy* (Fall 2017 Edition), ed. Edward N. Zalta, Uri Nodelman, Colin Allen, et. al., https://plato.stanford.edu/archives/fall2017/entries/justice/, accessed 4 October 2019.

3. Justice expects impartiality; similar cases warrant similar outcomes.
4. Justice and injustice require "an agent whose will alters the circumstances of its objects." In other words, direct harm done by natural causes cannot be an injustice, unless brought on by perhaps neglect of an agent.[3]

Many philosophers have made both similar and contradictory claims as to the meaning of justice, but for this study we move to the Judeo-Christian tradition, finding its foundation in biblical justice. *Economic Justice for All*, the 1986 pastoral letter issued by the United States Catholic Bishops, claimed that

> biblical justice is more comprehensive than subsequent philosophical definitions. It is not concerned with a strict definition of rights and duties, but with the rightness of the human condition before God and within society. Nor is justice opposed to love; rather, it is both a manifestation of love and a condition for love to grow.[4] (EJA, 39)

John Donahue stresses that biblical notions of justice and terms we now translate as such are broad and complex making it a "protean and many-faceted term."[5] He eventually settles on justice as "fidelity to the demands of a relationship."[6] Unlike our modern world, the Israelites presented in Scripture were "in a world where 'to live' is to be united with others in a social context either by the bonds of family or by covenant relationships."[7] Biblical justice assumes a network of relationships that move past utilitarian rights language. It is not enough to demand the bare minimum that American law, for example, requires of citizens. The Hebrew Scriptures operate as if Israelites had a covenantal obligation, even to the stranger among them. The constant emphasis on the least in

---

3. Miller, "Justice."

4. J. Alfaro, *Theology of Justice in the World* (Rome: Pontifical Commission on Justice and Peace, 1973), 40–41; E. McDonagh, *The Making of Disciples* (Wilmington, DE: Michael Glazier, 1982), 119.

5. John R. Donahue, SJ, "Biblical Perspectives on Justice," in *The Faith That Does Justice: Examining the Christian Sources for Social Change*, ed. John C. Haughey, SJ (Mahwah: Paulist Press, 1977), 68.

6. Donahue, "Biblical Perspectives on Justice," 69.

7. Donahue, 69.

society (i.e., the resident alien, the widow, the orphan) extended the cover of the covenant of the God of Abraham to virtually everyone an Israelite would meet. Walter Burghardt sums up what might be called the valued added by considering biblical justice:

> What is new in biblical justice? Ethical justice and legal justice, for all their significance, do not demand . . . love. Israel's God did. "You shall love your neighbor as yourself" (Lev 19:18). Even the stranger (Deut 10:19). Not a psychological balancing act: As much or as little as I love myself, so much or so little love must I lavish or trickle on others. No. I must love every other like another self, as if I were standing in their shoes, especially the paper-thin shoes of the downtrodden.[8]

If St. Thomas Aquinas as quoted in the *Catechism of the Catholic Church* is correct in describing love as the act of willing the good of another, then we can conclude that the Christian understanding of love makes justice and its demands constitutive to being a follower of Christ (CCC, 1766). Our fidelity to our relationship to the Triune God requires justice in every relationship. This includes our relationship to society and its relationship to us. The Christian vision prioritizes our relationship to the least among us: the stranger, the poor, children, and widows. That extends to all who find themselves on the periphery of society. They are us and we are them. Christian identification with the least is called solidarity, which Catholic social teaching states "must be seen above all in its value as a moral virtue that determines the order of institutions. On the basis of this principle the 'structures of sin' that dominate relationships between individuals and peoples must be overcome" (*Compendium of the Social Doctrine of the Church*, 193). In other words, not only must Christians work against personal sin, but also social sin. Racism, sexism, and classism, for example, are social sins that are antithetical to the Christian way of life. The proper response to any *ism*, to sin, or injustice is working for social justice.

---

8. Walter J. Burghardt, SJ, "Just Word and Just Worship: Biblical Justice and Christian Worship," *Worship* 73, no. 5 (September 1999): 390.

What Is Social Justice?

Social justice is the work of responding to the concerns of social sin—which systematically circumvents the possibility of a just society—through efforts to educate, advocate, and even legislate our way into a less unjust society. This commitment to work for justice and to respond to sin can be reached via reason by any person of good will, but is an imperative for the Christian. The *Compendium of the Social Doctrine of the Church* names social justice as "a requirement related to the social question which today is worldwide in scope, concerns the social, political and economic aspects and, above all, the structural dimension of problems and their respective solutions" (CSD, 201). Complex social problems, rooted in social sin, require individual recognition of our complicity, but also corporate, systemic social responses. These are the "proper answers" to the most "important social questions" that plague human societies: problems like, for example, increasing economic disparity, environmental racism, gender-based unequal pay, violence—sexual or otherwise—against transgender persons, and financial exploitation of undocumented immigrants, to name just a few (CSD, 81).

The biblical vision of the human person in community offers a perspective by which to judge the effectiveness of a society. Catholic social teaching does not offer us a preferred economic system, but it does offer us criteria by which to judge ours. Fidelity to the demands of a relationship extends to all relationships, including the networks that make up every society: family members, city residents, national citizens. That fidelity requires examination and recalibration, of not only personal patterns of behavior, but also our collective assumptions and the ways we respond to one another. Therefore, while Catholic social teaching "constantly calls for the most classical forms of justice to be respected: commutative, distributive and legal justice . . . ever greater importance has been given to social justice" (CSD, 201).

Ultimately, all efforts to live out the Gospel have as their end humanity's completeness and God's glorification. Justice work, if it is to be Christian, can never lose sight of this twofold end. Social systems, at their best, support human flourishing; they are not ends in themselves. That flourishing glorifies the God who created us. Paraphrasing St. Irenaeus, we can say, the glory of God is the human person fully alive.[9] Mark Searle rightly describes justice in its secular, legal context as "at best a bridle on evil"; however, the justice that Christian liturgy attempts to make manifest is "God's justice . . . the flowering of the good."[10] According to the biblical tradition, especially in reading the Hebrew and Christian Scriptures together, "a just society . . . [is] one marked by the fullness of love, compassion, holiness, and peace."[11] Jesus, the Just One, invites every Christian to become with, in, and through him, more than agents of justice, but a sacrament of his transformative presence in the world.

III

Liturgy: A School of the Self-Identity, Belonging, and Mission

In this section, we explore how liturgy forms persons as fully autonomous, yet interdependent, selves finding meaning and direction in community. We begin by looking at *Sancrosanctum concilium*, which says:

> The liturgy is the summit toward which the activity of the Church is directed; at the same time it is the font from which all her power flows. . . . In the reform and promotion of the liturgy, this full and active participation by all the people is the aim to be considered before all else. For it is the primary and indispensable source from which the faithful are to derive the true Christian spirit. (10, 14)

This clear and bold statement places liturgy at the center of Christian life. It truly is our source and summit. *Lumen gentium* connects the Church's very nature to the liturgy when it describes itself as "the visible sacrament of [Christ's] saving unity" (9). The Church is most clearly manifested in the world when it is at worship. That worship produces and forms Christians whose mission is to be the presence of God, the Body of Christ, for the life of the entire world.

---

9. See St. Irenaeus of Lyons, *Against Heresies: Book IV*, ch. 20, par. 7.

10 Mark Searle, "Serving the Lord with Justice," *Liturgy and Social Justice*, ed. Mark Searle (Collegeville, MN: Liturgical Press, 1980), 16.

11 Searle, "Serving the Lord with Justice," 16.

How then, does the liturgy form us for a life committed to justice? First, in the liturgical assembly the Christian is named. Each member is (1) made in the image and likeness of God; (2) separated from God because of original sin; and (3) redeemed and returned to God by the saving acts of Jesus Christ. Water, oil, fire, word, bread, and wine help to set the Christian apart for a sacred purpose. In the hearing and receiving of Scripture, Christians are posed with a set of questions about what is important for discipleship. Burghardt says that the "liturgy is not so much didactic as evocative."[12] The presence of Christ is evoked and we are confronted with his vision, his alternative way of relating to God and to others, and with the messiness of human relationships. In the gathered assembly, we are reminded of our brokenness, our incompleteness, and the longing for fullness of being. We are reminded of our search for fulfillment in ways that miss the mark (sin). We are reminded of our need for forgiveness, redemption, mercy, and just living. The proclamation of the Gospel attunes us to our "addictions and . . . illusions, casts a pitiless light on myopic self-interest, detaches [us] from a narrow selfishness, facilitates Christian discernment."[13]

Over time, the rituals of liturgy shape the way the Christian perceives herself or himself as an individual, as a member of the Body, and as an autonomous, yet interdependent person in the world. The moral, religious, and social imaginations of the individual and community are shaped by this repetition. For example, in every Eucharistic celebration, we acknowledge our incompleteness before God and the community; then, we listen to God's Word in history and for today; next, we respond with faith and petitions; then, we offer the one sacrifice for the life of the world; finally, we are sent forth to be the sacrament of Christ for all whom we encounter, finding him in those we serve once again. Through the liturgy, especially our Eucharistic sharing, we receive an incalculable gift back in return to encourage and sustain us in the mission.

When Jesus asks the disciples—and therefore us—who we think he is, we are also being given the chance to define ourselves. Upon reflection, we discover that we are loved sinners; we are

---

12. Burghardt, "Just Word and Just Worship," 395.
13. Burghardt, 394–395.

creatures given the privilege and grace of co-creation. We are fundamentally freed to be ourselves. This gift only comes through cycles of growing self-knowledge and acceptance. The rituals of liturgy not only dispose us to this way of perceiving things, like the classical definition of sacrament, they actually effect that change in us. The sacraments do what they say, and we become more and more of what we already are, the Body of Christ. Moreover, we are freed by this saving work. *Gaudium et spes* says, "In this way the church carries out its mission and in the very act it stimulates and advances human and civic culture, as well as contributing by its activity, including liturgical activity, to humanity's interior freedom" (58). And it is in that freedom that we have the capacity to be just, because we know who and whose we are. "To be just is to be open to the world as gift and to God as mystery."[14]

Kenosis

Liturgy, especially the Eucharist, opens us up to *kenosis*.[15] This is the love that the biblical tradition calls Christians into. We are called into love, an act of self-gift, of emptying out the self. In the Eucharist, the Kingdom of God breaks through and into our world, giving us a real taste of the fullness that is to come, and we are fed so that we can, in turn, feed a hungry world with our lives. We are given God's grace, if we are willing to receive it, to empty ourselves for the life of the world. Scripture teaches the following:

> Do nothing from selfish ambition or conceit, but in humility regard others as better than yourselves. Let each of you look not to your own interests, but to the interests of others. Let the same mind be in you that was in Christ Jesus,
>
> who, though he was in the form of God,
> did not regard equality with God
> as something to be exploited,

14. Donahue, 71.

15. *Kenosis*, from biblical Greek, is "a theological term for the 'self-emptying' of Jesus Christ in which he took the form of a slave or servant ... to accomplish the work of salvation through his death and resurrection (Phil. 2:5–11)." Donald K. McKim, *Westminster Dictionary of Theological Terms*, 1st ed. (Louisville, KY: Westminster John Knox Press, 1996), 153.

but emptied himself,
taking the form of a slave,
being born in human likeness.
And being found in human form,
he humbled himself
and became obedient to the point of death—
even death on a cross. (Philippians 2:3–8)

This is the vision of "justice-making" for which Christians are formed. It is a vision that relies wholly on the love and power of God to fuel every choice and campaign for change, knowing that it will require from us all that we have. It requires hope in things that cannot be seen. Scholars believe the above passage is an ancient Christian hymn that early Christian assemblies may have sung. St. Paul probably learned it during his visits. The ancient principle *lex orandi, lex credendi* speaks directly to our topic: the rule of prayer is the rule belief. Bernice Johnson Reagon, as quoted by Joseph A. Brown, connects *lex orandi, lex credendi* through the African American traditions of both worship and social justice:

> Reagon teaches us to value the power of the music when she encourages congregational singing as a way of social transformation: "Songs are a way to get to singing, though singing is what you're aiming for. And the singing is running sound through your body. You cannot sing a song and not change your condition."[16]

Reagon and Brown offer a liturgical spirituality that presumes that not only is the individual worshiper changed by singing and praying, but also the praying community is transformed and reoriented toward the justice of God. The Church's convictions about the Eucharist become much clearer: "The Eucharist commits us to the poor" (CCC, 1397). The rule of prayer is the rule of belief . . . is the rule of life: *lex orandi, lex credendi, lex vivendi.*

---

16. Joseph A. Brown, SJ, *To Stand on the Rock: Meditations on Black Catholic Identity* (Maryknoll: Orbis Books, 1998), 168. Brown clarifies that the physiological and psychological changes involved in "running sound through your body" can lead to spiritual renewal.

IV

No single American has done more to connect the Church's liturgical theology to Catholic social teaching than Virgil Michel. The pre-Vatican II Benedictine literary scholar and founding editor of *Orate Fratres* (later *Worship*) once put it most succinctly: "The liturgy is the indispensable basis of Christian social regeneration."[17] Thus, it would be appropriate to evaluate our current liturgical spirituality and practice by asking if this is in fact true. Regeneration? Social transformation? Is this how we perceive and perhaps experience Catholic Christian worship?

As we conclude this essay, we return to two perennial pastoral questions. First, do our liturgies actually form us for being just and doing justice? In our liturgies, have we been named, blessed, encouraged, admonished, reconciled, fed, and sent forth to promote truth and reconciliation in the world? Have we received and perceived our baptismal call to make all things new, including the very social order that formed us, in Christ Jesus? If not, we who lead and minister at the Church's worship have work to do. Second, are our liturgies in and of themselves experiences of justice? When we gather, do the practices, rubrics, and traditions of Catholic Christian liturgy mirror and embody the justice of the God we worship? We must honestly and faithfully examine our practice and observe who is excluded and why. We must wrestle with hard questions about what the rule of prayer teaches us about ourselves. There will not be easy answers or quick fixes, for we belong to a tradition that takes its worship seriously and change should be methodical and sometimes slow. And yet it is our work to do. The key here is to never forget who and whose we are, trusting, like the writers of "Lift Every Voice and Sing," that the God of weary years and silent tears will keep us on the path, as we pray:

> God of our weary years, God of our silent tears,
> thou who has brought us thus far on the way;
> thou who has by thy might, led us into the light,
> keep us forever in the path, we pray.[18]

---

17. Virgil Michel, OSB, "The Liturgy, the Basis of Social Regeneration," *Orate Frates* 9, (November 1935):

18. Johnson, 291.

Questions for Discussion:

1. Mark Searle says, "a just society . . . [is] one marked by the fullness of love, compassion, holiness, and peace." How is a "just society" made visible in the parish? In my neighborhood? In my family?

2. Virgil Michel, OSB, says, "The liturgy is the indispensable basis of Christian social regeneration." What in the community needs regeneration? How does the celebration of the liturgy awaken and strengthen a parish community to be the sacrament of Christ in their neighborhood? How do the hymns we sing, the homily, and the prayers animate (and form) us for mission?

3. Identify the ways in which the parish community (or family, choir) is actively present and engaged in the wider community. How has this involvement called the whole social system to conversion and renewal? Now identify those areas within the neighborhood the parish community has struggled to engage. What holds the parish back? What can inspire social action connected to the Gospel?

6 The *Ars Celebrandi* and Beauty

MICHAEL S. DRISCOLL

The *ars celebrandi*, "the art of proper celebration," is an important way to foster the participation of the People of God in the liturgy. Celebrating the liturgy properly is a skill and an art. It seeks to allow Christ to be the artist, the one who is active in the Eucharist, so that our participation becomes a sharing in his actions, his prayer, and in his offering. Certainly, the art of celebrating should be of major importance to priests who preside at the liturgy, but it also extends to all the liturgical ministers and even to the praying assembly.

During the last three pontificates, the particular question of beauty has been raised in a special way. First, John Paul II in his *Letter to Artists* (1999)[1] speaks as a poet, playwright, and actor to other artists about the key role they play in helping people find God through artistic beauty. His successor Benedict XVI addressed the role of beauty as the *veritatis splendor* on several occasions and especially in his apostolic exhortation following the synod on the

1. John Paul II, *Letter to Artists*, 3: "The theme of beauty is decisive for a discourse on art. It was already present when I stressed God's delighted gaze upon creation. In perceiving that all he had created was good, God saw that it was beautiful as well. . . . It is in living and acting that man establishes his relationship with being, with the truth and with the good. The artist has a special relationship to beauty. In a very true sense it can be said that beauty is the vocation bestowed on him by the Creator in the gift of 'artistic talent.' And, certainly, this too is a talent which ought to be made to bear fruit, in keeping with the sense of the Gospel parable of the talents (cf. *Mt* 25:14–30)."

Eucharist.[2] Finally, Pope Francis in his encyclical *Evangelii gaudium*, focuses on "the way of beauty (*via pulchritudinis*)" (167). It is significant that at the highest levels of the Church, there is a profound recognition that beauty is a significant way in which people encounter God. Our point of departure then is Francis' encyclical, *Evangelii gaudium*:

> Every form of catechesis would do well to attend to the "way of beauty" (*via pulchritudinis*). Proclaiming Christ means showing that to believe in and to follow him is not only something right and true, but also something beautiful, capable of filling life with new splendor and profound joy, even in the midst of difficulties. Every expression of true beauty can thus be acknowledged as a path leading to an encounter with the Lord Jesus. This has nothing to do with fostering an aesthetic relativism which would downplay the inseparable bond between truth, goodness and beauty, but rather a renewed esteem for beauty as a means of touching the human heart and enabling the truth and goodness of the risen Christ to radiate within it. If, as Saint Augustine says, we love only that which is beautiful, the incarnate Son, as the revelation of infinite beauty, is supremely lovable and draws us to himself with bonds of love. So a formation in the *via pulchritudinis* ought to be part of our effort to pass on the faith. Each particular Church should encourage the use of the arts in evangelization, building on the treasures of the past, but also drawing upon the wide variety of contemporary expressions so as to transmit the faith in a new "language of parables." We must be bold enough to discover new signs and new symbols, new flesh to embody and communicate the word, and different forms of beauty, which are valued in different cultural settings, including those unconventional modes of beauty, which may mean little to the evangelizers, yet prove particularly attractive for others. (167)

---

2. Benedict XVI, *Sacramentum caritatis*, 35: "Like the rest of Christian Revelation, the liturgy is inherently linked to beauty: it is *veritatis splendor*."

Here Pope Francis establishes beauty as one of the transcendentals, actually naming them as such: the true, the good, and the beautiful.[3] In so doing, he hints at the fourth transcendental—the One who is God. He is also establishing the relationship between them and even suggests how they work in tandem, beginning with the beautiful to lead to the good, the true, and ultimately to the One. The natural sequential order is to use the beauties of the earth as steps along which to mount upwards for the sake of that other beauty: from fair forms to fair practices, and from fair practices to fair notions until he arrives at the idea of absolute beauty. Further on in the encyclical, the pontiff again raises the idea of the transcendentals as beginning with beauty and ultimately leading to God.[4] All people have access to these, thus all people have access to God notwithstanding their religious tradition. However, for Christians beauty is what leads us through Christ to God.

---

3. St. Thomas Aquinas wrote of three transcendentals, namely *unum*, *bonum*, and *verum*, or the one, the good, and the true, which he referred to as the Most Real Being. St. Bonaventure added the term *pulchrum* or the beautiful to the list. In the fifteenth century in Florence, Italy, Marsilio Ficino was instrumental in reviving an interest in Plato and translating some of Plato's rediscovered texts. It is to Ficino that we can safely attribute the first definitive formulation of beauty, goodness, and truth, and this is found in his *Commentaries on Plato's Dialogues*. The idea was not without influence and in Palladio's *I Quattro Libri*, to take an example from architecture, is a reference to the "true, good and beautiful method of building." Even in the eighteenth century, the great philosophers of the enlightenment were well acquainted with the group of terms. Immanuel Kant's three great books, *Critique of Pure Reason* (1781), *Critique of Practical Reason* (1786), and *Critique of Judgment* (1790), dealt with the problems of truth, goodness, and beauty respectively. Truth was set out in terms of the categorical relations of predication and the syllogism; Goodness was defined in terms of the causal or even hypothetical relations arising from one's actions; and beauty in terms of the disjunctive relation between sense and color, for example, or those relations found in the contemplation of form and proportion. Hegel, drawing on the transcendental dialectic of Kant, introduced a complex system of sets of three among which can be found the group goodness, truth, and beauty. Later in the nineteenth century in America, Charles Sanders Peirce developed a logic of relatives and investigated many sets of threes corresponding in varying degrees to beauty, goodness, and truth. In fact, it might be concluded that Plato's original sequence for the group of terms was reinforced when Peirce thought that logic follows ethics and both follow aesthetics. Some suggest that there has been little development of these ideas of philosophy since the nineteenth century. Indeed, Nietzsche at the end of that century rejected consideration of the group rather questionably as being "unworthy of a philosopher." Yet the proliferation of twentieth century opinions dismissing the transcendentals as a serious theory in philosophy did elicit a number of influential philosophers, such as G. K. Chesterton, Edith Stein, and C. S. Lewis, whose writings develop and repropose truth, beauty, and goodness as the universal aspirations of humanity, which seeks an infinite good. As such, they assert, transcendentals help human beings undergo suffering and death with hope.

4. See *Evangelii gaudium*, 257.

When John Paul II wrote his *Letter to Artists* (Easter, 1999), he was writing as an artist in his own right both as a playwright and an actor. It is addressed "to all who are passionately dedicated to the search for new 'epiphanies' of beauty so that through their creative work as artists they may offer these as gifts to the world." In this letter, the Pope discussed the "special vocation" of the artist by beginning with the unique relationship between the artist and the creator. While God is the ultimate creator of all that is good and beautiful, with loving regard, the divine Artist (God) passes on to human artists a divine spark of God's own surpassing wisdom, calling them to share in God's creative power. Indeed, it was the pope's hope that all artists might receive in abundance the gift of that creative inspiration which is the starting point of every true work of art. Although the vocation of the artist is difficult, it is also necessary because the world desperately needs the beautiful. Thus, the artist is commissioned with this special vocation to bring beauty into the world and thereby promote the good. In doing so, the artist enriches the cultural heritage of each nation and of all humanity.

During my first year in the major seminary, I confided to my spiritual director that I judged that I had had more religious experiences in the concert hall than in the chapel. He told me not to worry; this would pass. I think he thought that I was confessing (my sins); rather I was professing (my beliefs), and, no, it did not pass! Forty some years later I do not think that I am so categorical to oppose the concert hall to the chapel, but I still believe that the arts, especially music, are a potent force for encountering the Transcendent. Years later, I discovered a book written by the now retired bishop of Poitiers, Albert Rouet,[5] who gave me language to explain what I was feeling. He goes beyond the idea of liturgy as being simply artful to the notion that the liturgy is an art form unto itself. Thus, liturgy uses other art forms, but to the degree that it is its own art form, we might compare it to opera. Like opera, which joins vocal and instrumental music, poetry, dance, and theatre, so too the liturgy makes use of many art forms to become a sacred work or an *opera sacra*.

---

5. Albert Rouet, *Liturgy and the Arts*, trans. P. Philibert (Collegeville, MN: Liturgical Press, 1997).

Bishop Rouet demonstrates how art and liturgy, when they join forces, express transcendence.

Of course, the most critical element for the *ars celebrandi* is well-celebrated rites. What does it mean to celebrate the rites well? What are the criteria that we use to judge? To celebrate the liturgy well requires doing the action and praying the liturgical texts so beautifully that their meaning clearly emerges in an intelligible and compelling manner. Because liturgical signs are vehicles of communication and instruments of faith, they should be simple, accessible, and intelligible. In short, they must be humanly attractive. In a word, if the rites are to be fully effective, we must tend to the aesthetics of worship. Suffice it to say that *good* liturgy is an absolute prerequisite to rich symbolic participation and contemplation. Because liturgy deals so much with symbols, it opens our imagination to multiple layers of interpretation. But symbols can be destroyed when they are interpreted, no longer as symbols, but as laws to be followed slavishly. Good liturgy should not be reduced to rubrics. That the liturgy is symbolic, however, does not mean that one can just do with it what one wants. It follows its own logic, thus there are liturgical norms to be taken into consideration. The most important point about liturgy is that it must be symbolically the bearer of the transcendent and as such, it relates to both the divine and the human. In the recent past, there was a tendency to translate the word liturgy from the Greek *leitourgia* (from *laos,* meaning "people," and *ergon,* meaning "work") as the "work of the people." A corrective must be added to emphasize that liturgy is also the work of God. The initiative must always originate on the side of God and worship is the human response to God's initiative. Therefore, liturgy is both an *opus Dei* and an *opus hominum.*[6]

Patrick Collins has named this phenomenon well when he invites us to understand ritual as an art. He writes,

> As such . . . [ritual] resembles drama, dance, music and poetry. Like drama, ritual enacts a story. It plays out the continuing saga of God's dealings with people which includes past, present and future dimensions. Like music, ritual has innate rhythms. Each moment prepares for the

6. A "work of God" and a "work of the people."

> next and each element flows out of what precedes. Again, like music, ritual involves the building of tensions and resolutions through the use of sounds and silence which create an aural experience of passage. Like dance, ritual involves movement becoming gesture, i.e., movement with symbolic meaning, such as processions, upraised hands, the laying on of hands, and eating and drinking. Like poetry, ritual uses words, not for explanation and communicating knowledge, but for exploration and creating insight into truth.[7]

But there is a cautionary note that although the liturgy has a performative quality, it is not a performance that would render the assembly as passive spectators. This would run against the foundational principle of *Sacrosanctum concilium,* which promotes full, conscious, and active participation of all the baptized. Nevertheless, there remains an element to which we must attend, namely the artful celebration.

When we speak of beauty, it can be of different kinds: natural and artistic. Let us set aside natural beauty in our focus on artistic beauty, especially as it relates to music. It is interesting that Pope Francis expresses a reservation about aesthetic relativism in much the same way as his predecessor.[8] The concern here is not beauty for the sake of beauty, but how beauty can be alluring to bring one to Christ and ultimately to God. John Paul expressed a similar concern that beauty, whether natural or artistic, creates a yearning within us that points to a transcendent Being and can only be satisfied by God.[9] In a similar fashion Benedict XVI has, repeatedly, emphasized that

---

7. Patrick Collins, *Bodying Forth: Aesthetic Liturgy* (New York and Mahwah: Paulist Press, 1992), 32.

8. Benedict XVI, in *Sacramentum caritatis*, 35, speaks to the Beauty that saves. He writes: "The liturgy is a radiant expression of the paschal mystery, in which Christ draws us to himself and calls us to communion. . . . This is no *mere aestheticism*, but the concrete way in which the truth of God's love in Christ encounters us, attracts us and delights us, enabling us to emerge from ourselves and drawing us towards our true vocation, which is *love*." Emphasis mine.

9. *Letter to Artists*, 16: "Beauty is a key to the mystery and a call to transcendence. It is an invitation to savor life and to dream of the future. That is why the beauty of created things can never fully satisfy. It stirs that hidden nostalgia for God which a lover of beauty like Saint Augustine could express in incomparable terms: 'Late have I loved you, beauty so old and so new: late have I loved you!'"

the *via pulchritudinis*,[10] the way of beauty, constitutes a privileged path by which one encounters God. But in his writings on the liturgy and the arts, one can see that Benedict's theology of beauty is hardly one of a mere aestheticism concerned with the technical perfection of art to the neglect of charity. It is an encounter with beauty that leads to action. John Paul II was also insistent on the connection between beauty and action. Citing the Polish poet Cyprian Norwid, he wrote, "beauty is to enthuse us for work, and work is to raise us up."[11]

A word must be said about the distinction between the beautiful and the pretty. There might be a tendency to confuse the beautiful with the pretty. But the distinction is that beauty contains within it the idea of truth. Sometimes we might surround ourselves with pretty objects, but in time, we cease to notice them because they are purely decorative. Rather than awakening our appetites to the beautiful, they may dull them. After a time we see them no longer. It is like wallpaper that is simply a background—nothing more. The beautiful on the other hand awakens us to the world. It does this to the degree that it speaks truthfully. An example from the visual arts that comes to mind is Pablo Picasso's painting, *Guernica*. The title refers to the city that was bombed by Nazi planes during the Spanish Civil War. The painting depicts the horrors of war and, as a result, has come to be an antiwar symbol and a reminder of the tragedies of war. It is not pretty by anyone's estimation, but it is beautiful in that it speaks to truth. In the musical arts, we might make the distinction between Muzak® (elevator music) and real music. If the music is simply background noise, does it really awaken us to anything? Or does it render us somnolent? John Paul calls this *kalokagathia* or beauty-goodness.[12] Beauty then is likened to both truth and

---

10. For further discussion of beauty as it applies to music, see Carolyn Pirtle, "The Via Pulchritudinis, Fauré's Requiem, and the Eucharist," *Logos: A Journal of Catholic Thought and Culture*, 19.2 (Spring 2016): 127–149.

11. Cited in *Letter to Artists*, part 3, in the section entitled "The artistic vocation in the service of beauty," par. 3.

12. John Paul II, in his *Letter to Artists*, says in note 4: "The Greek translation of the Septuagint expresses this well in rendering the Hebrew term *t(o)b* (good) as *kalón* (beautiful)." In paragraph 3 of the letter, he states: "The link between good and beautiful stirs fruitful reflection. In a certain sense, beauty is the visible form of the good, just as the good is the metaphysical condition of beauty. This was well understood by the Greeks who, by fusing the two concepts, coined a term which embraces both: *kalokagathía*, or beauty-goodness."

goodness. If something is truly beautiful, it speaks truth and leads to the good.

Ultimately, the beauty that saves is God's beauty; in God, truth, beauty, and goodness are a single matter. And whoever does something good, does at the same time something beautiful, as is said in French: *un beau geste*. Pope Benedict XVI turns to the French philosopher Simone Weil, who understood the connection between God and beauty when she wrote, "In all that awakens within us the pure and authentic sentiment of beauty, there is, truly, the presence of God. There is a kind of incarnation of God in the world, of which beauty is the sign." Benedict continues:

> Beauty, whether that of the natural universe or that expressed in art, precisely because it opens up and broadens the horizons of human awareness, pointing us beyond ourselves, bringing us face to face with the abyss of Infinity, can become a path towards the transcendent, towards the ultimate Mystery, towards God.[13]

Over the past twenty-five years as I travel around the United States speaking about liturgical matters to interested but not necessarily theologically educated audiences, the two biggest concerns that I hear deal with homilies and music. The good news behind this is that people have had some good experiences in both regards, but they thirst for better quality in both. The American bishops recognized this yearning in the 2007 document *Sing to the Lord: Music in Divine Worship* (STL), where they state: "Faith grows when it is well expressed in celebration. Good celebrations can foster and nourish faith. Poor celebrations may weaken it." What prophetic words! The church has come a long way in a few short decades from an understanding of how the sacraments work *ex opere operato*[14] to a greater appreciation of "full, conscious, and active participation" (SC, 14) of all the baptized, as was desired and mandated by the Second Vatican Council. Furthermore, the experience of celebrating the rites well has not been lost on the people. They come to know what constitutes good liturgy, particularly as good ritual experiences have

---

13. Pope Benedict XVI, *Address to the Artists in the Sistine Chapel*, 21 November 2009.

14. If you merely say the correct words using the proper elements, then the sacrament was automatically effected.

transformed their lives, and many are in active search for liturgical celebrations that nourish their spiritual needs. But the bishops' statement prompts the question as to what constitutes "good celebrations"? What criteria are available by which one can judge whether a liturgical celebration is good or bad? Is it determined by the style of music or by the quality of preaching? Is good liturgy simply a matter of following rules?

The *ars celebrandi* (the art of proper celebration) therefore is "the primary way to foster the participation of the People of God in the sacred rite" (SacCar, 38). Celebrating the liturgy properly is a skill and an art. Directions and instructions for how Christians are to celebrate the Eucharist abound throughout Christian history, including the current edition of the *General Instruction of the Roman Missal* (GIRM).

In 2000, the third edition of *The Roman Missal* was published. Immediately work began to translate this large volume from Latin (*editio typica*) into the vernacular languages. The first order of business was the translation of the 2002 GIRM by the International Committee on English in the Liturgy (ICEL). In 2003, the US bishops published this document in the *Liturgy Documentary Series*,[15] with a beautiful cover featuring the painting of *The Adoration of the Lamb* by Jan van Eyck. In the same year, a book appeared in French entitled *L'art de célébrer*.[16] The essential difference is that the English edition presented the GIRM without commentary whereas the French publication, as the title suggests, was a pastoral guide intended to help in the artful celebration of the liturgy.

In some circles the English edition was received as purely a legal text, a how-to-do book. If good celebrations were simply a matter of following rules, sometimes called a rubrical approach, then there would be good liturgy everywhere. But good celebrations require more than simply coloring within the lines. Good celebrations require an artful sense. At the eleventh Synod of Bishops dealing with the Eucharist (October 2005), three sorts of concerns were addressed: theological (doctrine and catechetical), ethical, and

15. *General Instruction of the Roman Missal. Liturgy Documentary Series* 2. Washington, DC: United States Conference of Catholic Bishops, 2003.

16. Centre national de pastorale liturgique, *L'art de célébrer: Guide Pastoral* [The art of celebrating: A pastoral guide] (Paris: Editions du Cerf, 2003).

aesthetical. That the bishops were concerned about doctrinal and ethical aspects of the Eucharist does not come as any great surprise, but their expressed concern about the *ars celebrandi* marks a new-found interest in how the liturgy is celebrated beautifully. In his postsynodal exhortation, *Sacramentum caritatis*, Pope Benedict XVI explores this last dimension:

> In the course of the Synod, there was frequent insistence on the need to avoid any antithesis between the *ars celebrandi*, the art of proper celebration, and the full, active and fruitful participation of all the faithful. The primary way to foster the participation of the People of God in the sacred rite is the proper celebration of the rite itself. The *ars celebrandi* is the best way to ensure their *actuosa participatio*. The *ars celebrandi* is the fruit of faithful adherence to the liturgical norms in all their richness. (38)

Perhaps there is no aspect so important in the whole discussion of the transcendent and symbolic nature of liturgy as the role of the aesthetic experience or the *ars celebrandi*.

The Church has always felt the importance of the artful element in the liturgical celebration. The aesthetic experience can be the instrument that assists the faithful to make the assent of faith. It is in the liturgy where we encounter the divine through the beauty of the rites, music, art, and architecture. Therefore, reducing the liturgy to a series of rubrics would be a grave mistake. An overly rubrical approach can lead to dead symbols and will fail to stir the faith in those celebrating. Students of the liturgy, particularly seminarians, need to be schooled in this more artful approach. Moreover, all liturgical ministers who prepare liturgies of all kinds need to know for proper, artful celebration. Attention to the *ars celebrandi* should be a primary focus for parish priests, deacons, pastoral associates, liturgists, music directors, teachers, catechists, and any other parish staff members responsible for the preparation of the liturgy, to help them craft beautiful celebrations.

Questions for Discussion:

1. Identify an event or several events when you encountered the presence of God within the beauty of nature, in the arts, or in the liturgy. How did you experience God? What did you learn about God, Church, and self?
2. Why are well planned and executed liturgical celebrations so important for the liturgy to achieve its full result and bring about the greatest spiritual fruits?
3. Why does good liturgy require more than simply coloring within the lines (rubrical approach) and demand an artful sense (*via pulchritudinis*)?

7 The Prayer of Life between Source and Summit

RODICA STOICOIU

Introduction

Before Paul wrote:

> For I received from the Lord what I also handed on to you, that the Lord Jesus on the night when he was betrayed took a loaf of bread, and when he had given thanks he broke it and said, "This is my body that is for you. Do this I remembrance of me." In the same way he took the cup also, after supper, saying, "This cup is the new covenant in my blood. Do this, as often as you drink it, in remembrance of me." For as often as you eat this break and drink the cup, you proclaim the Lord's death until he comes.
> (1 Corinthians 11:23–26)

Before the first Gospel described:

> While they were eating, he took a loaf of bread, and after blessing it he broke it, gave it to them, and said, "Take; this is my body." Then he took a cup, and after giving thanks he gave it to them, and all of them drank from it. He said to them, "This is my blood of the covenant, which is poured out for many." (Mark 14:22–24)

Before there were letters or Gospels, the Church gathered on the first day of the week and told the story of Jesus; we prayed for one another and we celebrated the Eucharist. The liturgy formed and shaped the Church from its beginning. And before all other Christian spiritualties arose, the liturgy supplied the foundation for spirituality. The liturgy drew us into the paschal mystery, imbued us with the Spirit, and shaped our life and purpose.

What was true then, is true now. "In him we live and move and have our being" (Acts 17:28). We are a people shaped by our communal prayer. When the Church gathers in prayer, we are immersed into the very life, death, and Resurrection of Christ. As missionary disciples, each of us is called to live out the paschal mystery in our day-to-day activity. Thus, we fulfill the mission of our Baptism: to call the world to God, who is the heart of the world, and to build up God's Kingdom.

The journey of every Christian is a process of becoming. Liturgical experience and prayer shape this process of *becoming*; it is manifest in the midst of community. We express our relationship with God and one another through symbol and ritual. Altogether, over time, we are formed ever more fully into the relational being that was established through our Baptism. Hence, liturgical spirituality fashions our ontological reality. It molds our being. Through our public worship we develop a way of being human, both as a celebrating community, but also as persons in the world that "see" all of creation in light of the paschal mystery. This is so instilled into us that when we answer the call of Matthew 25:35–40—

> [F]or I was hungry and you gave me food, I was thirsty and you gave me something to drink, I was a stranger and you welcomed me, I was naked and you gave me clothing, I was sick and you took care of me, I was in prison and you visited me. . . . Just as you did it to one of the least of these . . . you did it to me"

—we are living out a liturgical spirituality. Dr. Paul Ford recapitulates this saying, "A *lived* liturgy is all the spirituality one needs."[1]

---

1. Paul F. Ford, "Lived Liturgy, First Spirituality," *Liturgical Ministry* 10 (Fall 2001): 186.

The Language of Liturgical Spirituality

The language of liturgical spirituality is the language of liturgical experience; it is a language of symbol and ritual. Liturgical experience encompasses all forms of the public prayer of the Church, which includes each sacrament, the Liturgy of the Hours, the seasons of the liturgical year, and rites such as funerals and the blessing of an engaged couple.

For most people, their primary formative liturgical experience is the weekly sacramental encounter of the Eucharist, even though they may occasionally celebrate liturgies of Baptism, Marriage, or funerals. It is important to note that these celebrations unfold within the rhythm of the liturgical seasons (i.e., Advent, Christmas, Lent, Triduum, Easter, and Ordinary Time), which inform and shape one's liturgical spirituality. Participation in these celebrations sensitizes us to specific ways of marking relationships, time, life, and death. Indeed, the repetitive, immersive nature of liturgy develops a spirituality that transforms human experience in light of the mystery of God. That is to say, through symbol and ritual encounter, what is very human (e.g., food and drink, water and oil) becomes an invitation into the life of God in our midst. The practice of liturgy slowly changes our experience of the world around us, as the "stuff" of human existence become entry points into the divine.

Specifically, symbols invite us to encounter God in a very real and intimate way. They do not define, they evoke. They are not explicit, but rather, they are ambiguous. Their meanings are never exhausted. They are action as well as object, food to eat, wine to drink, oil to pour, water that can cleanse, but also drown. They are dangerous, and by embracing them, we, the Church, are forever changed. Only because they speak to us first as human beings, can these rich symbols invite us into God's life. Consider, every time you make the Sign of the Cross, for example, some aspect of the paschal mystery is revealed. These tangibles, these signs, symbols, and rituals all lead us to a profound encounter with the paschal mystery of Christ.

The ambiguity of liturgical language is purposeful. It embraces speech, action, and object, and rather than define reality, it discloses presence. Consider the open-ended nature of the greeting at Mass: "The Lord be with you." This expresses a hope and an expression of faith that when two or more gather in Christ's name there he will be in their midst. Liturgical language speaks as profoundly of God's presence through silence as it does through proclamation. It is a language of patient waiting as well as a call to formation and change. In how we move, stand, process, sing, and sign, in all our ritual expression, we both communicate the reality of God and open ourselves to God's transformative love. We make ourselves vulnerable. In this way, liturgy is an exercise in trust. There could be danger here. We put our being at risk of change, yet that danger is mitigated because it is accomplished in love, within a community living in faith. Through these liturgical experiences with symbol and ritual, we are given a language by which we can interpret reality. Our understanding of what it means to be human changes. We "see" through the lens of the Gospels. And through this repeated participation of "being" this new creation, our spirituality is formed and nurtured. We relate to God and one another through this practice of presence that, over time, forms us into a way of being always and everywhere.

Liturgical spirituality is nourished by the liturgy, especially the Eucharistic liturgy that provides its center, but it is meant to be lived beyond the doors of the Church, in the lives of the community. Our ritual celebrations gather us, re-form us, and help us share the dangerous memory of Christ. By so doing, our liturgical spirituality guides our *becoming*. Liturgical spirituality is, therefore, an aspect of the "this" in the "do this in memory of me."

The Facets of Liturgical Spirituality—Stepping Stones to Being in Christ

Living Liturgy as Spirituality

Sacrosanctum concilium says, "[T]he liturgy is the summit toward which the activity of the Church is directed; at the same time it is the font from which all her power flows" (10). There is a clear expectation that out of liturgical celebration, human persons will be changed and this new reality will be implanted into their lives and be manifest through their daily, personal spirituality. Thus, the ground for liturgical spirituality to act and to change human life is in the space between *source* and *summit*. It is in the messy course of human experience where this appropriation of liturgical spirituality is lived out; our laughter and tears take on new purpose through the paschal mystery.[2] The constitution continues, "The liturgy in its turn moves the faithful, filled with 'the paschal sacraments,' to be 'one in holiness'" (10). Viewed from this perspective, *Sacrosanctum concilium*'s call for "full, conscious, and active participation" takes on even more importance (14).

How are we to be the ongoing symbolic encounter of Christ in the world, if we do not express this in our liturgical celebrations? How are we to live and breathe the spirituality of liturgy (i.e., the paschal mystery) in the missionary activity of our lives if we do not encounter the fullness of communal personhood in our celebrations? The vision of the Second Vatican Council is the vision of the early Christians mentioned above. The baptized faithful are to risk everything in order to become a new creation, one community in Christ. We find this notion of liturgical spirituality clearly presented in *Lumen gentium* (LG):

> "God is love, and they who abide in love abide in God, and God abides in them" (1 Jn 4:16). God has poured out his love in our hearts through the holy Spirit who has been given to us (see Rom 5:5); therefore the first and most necessary gift is charity, by which we love God above all things and our neighbor because of him. But if charity is to grow and like a good seed produce fruit in the soul, all of the faithful must willingly hear the word of God and carry out his will by what they do, with the help of his grace; they must frequently partake of the sacraments, especially the Eucharist, and take part in the liturgy; they must constantly apply themselves to prayer, self-denial, active sisterly and brotherly service and the practice of all the virtues. This is because love, as the bond of perfection and fullness of the law (see Col 3:14; Rom 13:10), directs and gives meaning to all the means of sanctification and leads them to their goal. Hence the true disciples of Christ are noted both for love of God and love of their neighbor. (42)

---

2 Jesus Castellano Cervers, OCD, "Liturgy and Spirituality," in *The Handbook for Liturgical Studies*, vol. 2, *Fundamental Liturgy*, ed. Anscar Chupungo, OSB (Collegeville, MN: Liturgical Press, 1997) 52.

It is clear that liturgical spirituality grows from communal liturgical experience par excellence.

Becoming in Christ: Baptism, Eucharist, and Liturgical Spirituality

Liturgical spirituality fully embraced expresses a very specific vision of being human. Genesis tells us that human beings are created in the image of God (Genesis 1:27). We believe in a Triune God, a God who in God's very self is a communion of persons.[3] As human beings, we carry this potentiality for communion within ourselves. This potentiality moves to actuality in the relations established by Baptism. In the dying and rising of Baptism, we enter into a new way of being as a communion of persons, an *ekklesia* or Church. To be baptized is to take our place in the Eucharistic community; it is to fulfill our personhood as a being-in-relation. Being a person in this understanding is essentially a relational concept. It is a movement outward from self, an *ekstasis*, a movement toward communion with God and one another. This is an existential reality, wherein through Baptism the individual becomes a person "so deeply and existentially" bound to the community that they have become a relational entity."[4] Each member of the baptized becomes a member of a communion of persons, the Church. In Baptism, we take on this ecclesial web of relationships modeled on those of the Trinity itself.[5]

If such an identity is established in Baptism, it is in the Eucharist that its fullness is expressed ecclesially. Here *eucharist* is understood as an action of a living assembly in which the person of Jesus Christ is encountered and expressed. It is here that our ecclesial personhood, our being, is manifest. We stand in openness to our God who communicates self through Word and Spirit in the inherently Trinitarian character of liturgy. As Church, we express our personhood as relational beings. We give ourselves away, no longer

3. Karl Rahner, *The Trinity*, trans. Joseph Donceel (London: Burnes and Oates, 1975), 109–111.

4. John Zizioulas, *Being as Communion* (Crestwood: St. Vladimir's Seminary Press, 1997), forward by John Meyendorff, 190.

5. Zizioulas, *Being as Communion*, 220.

isolated and alone, but living for others in the image of our God, three persons-in-communion, in the mystery of the Trinity.

Actualized in Baptism, manifested in the Eucharistic celebration, and communicated through time and space in symbol and ritual, liturgical spirituality must find purpose in our daily lives. In our actions toward others, our just response to the needs of the world, liturgical spirituality is our personal antiphon to the fullness of being expressed by the Church.

Liturgical Spirituality as Ongoing Conversion

"Fifty years after you were baptized you should be fifty years more really baptized than the day the water was poured on your head."[6] Deepening our liturgical spirituality is a lifelong dynamic of going forth from and returning to worship. The conversion process never ends; it is a *metanoia*, a constant turning towards God. Often, we think of conversion as the prelude to entry into the Church (i.e., for an inquirer or catechumen), as something new people experience, not as reality or truth that is part of our own spiritual life. However, it is true that initial conversion is found through the Spirit in evangelization as stated in the *Rite of Christian Initiation of Adults*:

> From evangelization, completed with the help of God, come the faith and initial conversion that cause a person to feel called away from sin and drawn into the mystery of God's love. The whole period of the precatechumenate is set aside for this evangelization, so that the genuine will to follow Christ and seek baptism may mature. (37)

It is also true that their conversion is united to our own and that this is marked through public celebration (RCIA, 41). As we witness their journey of faith unfold (e.g., reception into the Order of Catechumens, celebration of the scrutinies, dismissals from Mass), we may fail to realize that the liturgical rites themselves assume that the ongoing conversion of the baptized unfolds along with theirs! These public

6 Michael J. Himes, *The Mystery of Faith: An Introduction to Catholicism* (Cincinnati: Franciscan Media, 2004), 53.

liturgical rites call each of us to turn toward God, to renew our life in God.

Catechumens are to be "helped by the example and support of sponsors, godparents, and the entire Christian community" (RCIA, 75.2; see 9). As they grow in faith, their transition into the Christian life "should become manifest by means of its social consequences" (RCIA, 75.2). Their presence within a community of faith is clearly indicated. Their conversion is lived out in the midst of the community's conversion, in the midst of our daily prayer and support and through liturgical celebrations. "Provision should also be made for the entire community involved in the formation of the catechumens" (RCIA, 80). Through their participation in the life of the community, their nascent liturgical spirituality finds root and grows. Catechumens experience the manifestation of the Gospel as they share in the work of the parish community (see RCIA, 75.4).

In soup kitchens and food pantries, in visiting the sick, in breaking open the Word, liturgical spirituality embraces ongoing conversion in us all, witnessed by our actions to embody Christ in the world. The reality remains; conversion is a lifelong challenge for everyone. The process of conversion experienced by the catechumens teaches the baptized how to set aside that which does not lead to communion with God and "then strengthen all that is upright, strong, and good" (RCIA 141). This is the paschal mystery, which the liturgy helps us embody. Are we living in such a way that fifty years after our own Baptism we will truly be "fifty years more baptized?"

Liturgical Spirituality and the Grace of Time

As noted above, a liturgical spirituality is a process that develops over a lifetime. Now we turn to discuss the role of liturgical spirituality in the grace of time itself. We have established that liturgical spirituality is centered on the paschal mystery; so too is the Church's reckoning of time. As time is marked with the rising and setting of the sun, we reveal layers of meaning about the paschal mystery. Here are some examples of how the Church marks time: (a) prayer at appointed times throughout the day (Liturgy of the Hours), (b) celebrating the Resurrection of Christ at Sunday Mass, and (c) commemorating Christ's saving deeds over the course of a calendar year.[7]

At the heart of every Sunday and central to every feast is the celebration of Christ's paschal mystery. The Sunday feast celebrates one thing: the life, death, Resurrection, and Ascension of Christ and our life in him. We are always celebrating the one total mystery of Christ even though the liturgical year breaks down this reality into many aspects. In effect, we celebrate many facets of one truth. *Sacrosanctum concilium* reminds us that

> the Church is conscious that it must celebrate the saving work of the divine Bridegroom by devoutly recalling it on certain days throughout the course of the year. Every week, on the day which the Church has called the Lord's Day, it keeps the memory of the Lord's resurrection, which she also celebrates once in the year, together with his blessed passion, in the most solemn festival of Easter.
>
> Within the cycle of a year, moreover, the Church unfolds the whole mystery of Christ, from the incarnation and birth until his ascension, the day of Pentecost, and the expectation of blessed hope and of the Lord's return.
>
> Recalling thus the mysteries of redemption, the Church opens to the faithful the riches of the Lord's powers and merits, so that these are in some way made present in every age in order that the faithful may lay hold on them and be filled with saving grace. (102)

The Church's ordering of the days, seasons, and its observance of time is sacramental. We understand time as an invitation into the mystery of God mediated through Christ, through the Holy Spirit. The words spoken during the preparation of the paschal candle at the Easter Vigil highlights this reality:

---

7. See the *Universal Norms on the Liturgical Year and the General Roman Calendar* for a complete description.

Christ yesterday and today
the Beginning and the End
the Alpha
and the Omega
All time belongs to him
and all the ages
To him be the glory and power
through every age for ever. Amen.
(*The Roman Missal*, "The Easter Vigil," 11)

Even though God's Word revealed to us does not change, we know that we do because we are beings in time. Hence, as Christians, we have a specific orientation towards time, which is shaped by the liturgy and thus helps form our spirituality. We recognize that liturgical time provides the narrative by which we interpret our reality.

Liturgical Spirituality and Eternal Life

As I write this chapter, I sit at my mother's bedside. She will soon pass from this world, and a lifetime of liturgy is shaping her final journey. As with every other aspect we have discussed, the paschal mystery is central here once more. The *Order of Christian Funerals* (OCF) says:

> In the face of death, the Church confidently proclaims that God has created each person for eternal life and that Jesus, the Son of God, by his death and resurrection, has broken the chains of sin and death that bound humanity. Christ "achieved his task . . . principally by the paschal mystery of his blessed passion, resurrection from the dead, and glorious ascension." (1)

The Church's orientation towards sickness, death, and eternal life is steeped in the liturgy of the Church—in these rites, we are presented liturgical spirituality. Beginning with the Christian life in Baptism, fed at the table of the Eucharist, lived out through the cycles of hours and day and season, in feasts and fasts, the mystery of God breathes through our prayer. Whether we minister to those who are sick, to help return them to health "by showing love for the sick, and by celebrating the sacraments with them," or reach out to console the bereaved, we do all these actions in faith and hope in the resurrection that is grounded in the liturgy and lived out in life (OCF, 8). 'The Church calls each member of Christ's Body . . . to participate in the ministry of consolation: to care for the dying, to pray for the dead, to comfort those who mourn" (OCF, 8).

The symbols of the funeral rites (i.e., pall and candle, water and word) speak the vocabulary of our lives of faith. Even at a time when mourners may not consciously connect with the power of sacrament and symbol, through the support and prayer of the community, these actions and symbols carry the bereaved when they cannot carry themselves. It is the ultimate action of liturgical spirituality inculcated into our very being, that when we are unable to stand on our own, we are held fast by rite and sacrament, community and symbol until we have the strength to share in these again.

Over her last few days, she no longer spoke; my mother drew on a lifetime of liturgy in silent response as we prayed. She made the Sign of the Cross as she was anointed; she held out her hand to receive the Eucharist; in quiet, she listened with her whole being. Instilled in her being was the truth of the liturgy, a lifetime of rehearsal prepared her for this moment. In her faith was the witness that even when we are at our most frail, the actions and belief of a lifetime are expressive declarations of our relationship with God. When she breathed her last, in the calm hours of the morning, we who gathered around her body found comfort and strength in the familiarity of the gestures and prayers that marked every moment of a life of faith and which spoke of hope and the final surrender into the great mystery of Christ's life, death, and Resurrection.

Conclusion

We have explored the essence of liturgical spirituality as the natural response of our life of faith, living and breathing the action of the liturgy. Whether it is sacramental ritual, symbol, object or action, silence or singing, the facets of the paschal mystery that we celebrate as community are inscribed into our being in every moment of our lives. The rhythm of worship calls us to enter the dangerous memory of Christ in celebration and then go forth to be the mission of Christ in the world. Liturgical spirituality is formed within us through the liturgy, but it serves its greatest purpose as it shapes our being and actions between source and summit.

Liturgical spirituality instilled in our very self becomes the lens by which we interpret our reality. It is the hermeneutic of our life. Even as we, always and everywhere, celebrate the paschal mystery we draw on this spirituality to help us understand it, construe it, and enact it, one facet at a time. From the moment we die and rise in the waters of Baptism, to the moment we die and rise with Christ, liturgical spirituality defines our purpose, strengthens our resolve, and guides our actions as we build the Kingdom of God. We return regularly to the liturgy to remind ourselves who we are, but we do this always with the intent that we will go forth again to give ourselves away, to call others to Christ, to call the world to this fundamental truth of its heart.

Questions for Discussion:

1. Fr. Michael Himes says, "[F]ifty years after you were baptized you should be fifty years more really baptized then the day the water was poured on your head." What does he mean by this? Can you give some examples of what this might look like in your life?
2. Explain how symbols and ritual train and nurture our liturgical spirituality. Provide an example of how a specific symbolic action has formed your liturgical spirituality. What did you learn about God? About Christ? About the Church? About yourself?
3. We say that at the heart of liturgical spirituality is the paschal mystery. What does this mean for you? How might you explain this to a fellow parishioner who has not read this chapter?

8 Music in the Liturgy and Missionary Discipleship

FABIAN R. YANEZ

Introduction[1]

Even now, more than fifty years since the promulgation of *Sacrosanctum concilium* (SC), we are continuing to mine the riches of the Second Vatican Council,[2] especially as the documents pertain to liturgy and music. *Lumen gentium* (LG), for example, provides an enriched vision of the Church and its ministers. LG reminds us that "in the building up of Christ's body there is engaged a diversity of members and functions" (7; see also 10). Whether ordained, professed religious, or laity, all are called to celebrate in a spirit of full, conscious, and active participation (see SC 14). The liturgy of the Church is not a gathering of spectators, but of active participants in the priesthood of Christ according to each person's ontological role. Whether baptized or ordained, all of God's people are essential in the liturgical act.

1. Music ministers need to have this book within reach: *Sing to the Lord: Music in Divine Worship* (Pastoral Liturgy Series Book 4) © 2007 updated, United States Conference of Catholic Bishops (USCCB). I will refer to this resource throughout this essay, but please seek out the full instruction from this book. Also abbreviated as STL.

2. For example, in the mid-1970s, my mentor (Robert Igoe Blanchard, founder and executive director of the Composers' Forum for Catholic Worship, Inc.) told me that it would take fifty years before the Church in general would realize that the Second Vatican Council was more than just moving the furniture.

As we consider our liturgical celebrations in light of the Council, we are also moving beyond the physicality of the liturgy—that is, the ritual action—to exploring more deeply the interiority of the liturgy—that is, the reality of what the paschal mystery of Christ calls us to live. This reality transforms us as we go forth from our liturgical celebrations into the world. *Sing to the Lord: Music in Divine Worship* (STL), the US bishops' 2007 instruction on liturgical music, speaks directly to this reality: "The Paschal hymn, of course, does not cease when a liturgical celebration ends. Christ, whose praises we have sung, remains with us and leads us through church doors to the whole world" (8). Moreover, STL continues, "Charity, justice, and evangelization are thus the normal consequences of liturgical celebration. *Particularly inspired by sung participation,* the body of the Word Incarnate goes forth to spread the Gospel with full force and compassion" (9, emphasis added).

Music is indeed a "necessary" and "integral" part of how liturgy inspires and forms us for evangelization and missionary discipleship. This essay will explore the importance of music in liturgical celebrations, its effects on how we understand and live out the paschal mystery, and its role in forming the Church as missionary disciples. These topics are important not only for those directly involved in music ministry, but also for the whole parish community, who longs to grow in faith and be sent forth on mission.

The Importance of Music in Liturgical Celebrations

No one should ever be denied the gift of song; it is in our bones, a gift from the Creator. As STL 1–2 reminds us,

> God has bestowed upon his people the gift of song. God dwells within each human person, in the place where music takes its source. Indeed, God, the giver of song, is present whenever his people sing his praises.*

* "Do you not know that you are the temple of God, and that the Spirit of God dwells in you? If anyone destroys God's temple, God will destroy that person; for the temple of God, which you are, is holy" (1 Cor 3:16–17).

A cry from deep within our being, music is a way for God to lead us to the realm of higher things. †

People have been using this gift of song to praise God for centuries. *Sing to the Lord* (3–4) provides a succinct timeline of music's importance in Scripture, from the Israelites' song of freedom after passing through the Red Sea (Exodus 15:1–18, 21) to the songs and instruments of David's time (2 Samuel 6:5) to the hymns sung by Jesus and his apostles (Matthew 26:30, Mark 14:26) and St. Paul (Acts 16:25).

Our liturgical celebrations are a continuation of this tradition. Liturgical music unites the Church throughout all time. It is an echo of our ancestors in faith; it is the song of the present *ekklesia*, gathered on earth for the common purpose of giving praise and thanksgiving to God; it is a foretaste of the hymn that we hope to sing with "the host of Angels . . . in one chorus of exultant praise" (RM, Preface III of the Sundays in Ordinary Time). When we join in singing "Holy, Holy, Holy Lord God of hosts," it is hard to imagine any of the angels remaining mute. Why should it be any different when we gather for liturgy?

Every time we hear the Preface and sing the *Sanctus*, we are reminded that the heavenly liturgy is the template for the earthly liturgy, and the earthly liturgy is the template for the worship that we live in the modern world. The heavenly liturgy is celebrated in praise of God in solidarity with all the angels and saints, and the earthly liturgy is celebrated in praise of God with our worshiping communities. Every word and every note we sing unites us in solidarity with all humanity and all creation. Liturgical music, then, is important because its very nature reflects and demands that we live out that solidarity in the world.

Liturgical music is also important because it manifests both unity and diversity: the unity of the assembled Church and its diversity of ministries. A large portion of *Sing to the Lord* (15–47) details the unique musical roles and functions of the bishop, priest, deacon, assembly, choir, psalmist, cantor, organist, other instrumentalists, and director of music ministries. The role of the assembly, or

---

† See St. Augustine, Epis. 161, De origine animae hominis, 1, 2; PL XXXIII, 725, as quoted in Pope Pius XIII, Encyclical On Sacred Music *(Musicae Sacrae Disciplina)* (MSD), no. 5, www. vatican.va/holy_father/pius_xii/encyclicals/documents/hf_p-xii_enc_25121955_musicae-sacrae_en.html.

congregation,[3] is "especially important" (STL, 11) because "singing is one of the primary ways that the assembly of the faithful participates actively in the Liturgy" (STL, 26). The unity of the assembly's voice should be full and robust, particularly when singing in responsive dialogues with the priest (STL, 19, 21), deacon (STL, 23), choir (STL, 29), psalmist (STL, 34–36), and cantor (STL, 37). With their responsive nature, these dialogues make musically incarnate the diversity of the Church's different ministerial roles and the unity of the entire Body of Christ, gathered as one in the liturgy. When the Church sings together, we follow the injunction of St. Paul to the Colossians: we "let the word of Christ dwell in [us] richly, as in all wisdom [we] teach and admonish one another, singing psalms, hymns, and spiritual songs with gratitude in [our] hearts to God" (Colossians 3:16). We profoundly preach the word and sacrament with one another, to one another, for the spiritual benefit of one another.

In order for our liturgical celebrations to bear this spiritual fruit, the use of music must be effective. As *Sing to the Lord* counsels:

> Faith grows when it is well expressed in celebration. Good celebrations can foster and nourish faith. Poor celebrations may weaken it. Good music "make[s] the liturgical prayers of the Christian community more alive and fervent so that everyone can praise and beseech the Triune God more powerfully, more intently and more effectively." (STL, 5, quoting *Music sacra disciplina*, 31; see also MSD, 33)

With music having such great importance in our liturgical celebrations, it requires both beautiful and intentional celebration and careful planning in order to be effective. Worship is not entertainment. Pastoral musicians and liturgists are not creating art for the sake of art; rather, they are leaders of prayer, doing everything in a spirit of humility. Pastoral ministers put aside their vainglory, anxieties, tiredness, and distractedness in order to do everything out of love for God's people. Musicians must remember to allow time for

---

3. Recently, I have noticed that there is often a preference for the word "assembly," based on the Greek ἐκκλησία. This is scriptural. However, I also enjoy the word "congregation," based on the Latin *congregatio*. The prefix *con* means "with," and the root word *grex* means, "flock." Both terms, "assembly" and "congregation," imply a communal action.

communal silence, which provides an invitation to contemplate the mystery that we celebrate and whose importance "cannot be overemphasized" (STL, 118).[4] This interplay between music, silence, and many other symbols and actions all contribute to the liturgical celebration being a "kind of ritual art" (STL, 123), but always with the intent of helping "the members of the gathered assembly . . . to give voice to the gift of faith" (STL, 125).

To this end, all music chosen for liturgical celebrations should be selected in accordance with the three judgments introduced by *Music in Catholic Worship* in 1972 and restated in *Sing to the Lord,* 126–136. These judgments are as follows:

> **The Liturgical Judgment**: Is this [musical] composition capable of meeting the structural and textual requirements set forth by the liturgical books for this particular rite? (STL, 127)
>
> **The Pastoral Judgment**: This takes into consideration the actual community gathered to celebrate in a particular place at a particular time. Does a musical composition promote the sanctification of the members of the liturgical assembly by drawing them closer to the holy mysteries being celebrated? Does it strengthen their formation in faith by opening their hearts to the mystery being celebrated on this occasion or in this season? Is it capable of expressing the faith that God has planted in their hearts and summoned them to celebrate? (STL, 130)
>
> **The Musical Judgment**: The musical judgment asks whether this musical composition has the necessary aesthetic qualities that can bear the weight of the mysteries celebrated in the Liturgy. Is it technically, aesthetically, and expressively worthy? (STL, 134)

4. Even the hymns we sing, such as "Let All Mortal Flesh Keep Silence" and "You Are Mine" (David Haas, GIA), form and inform us to observe and appreciate the gift of silence at the appropriate times in worship.

When these judgements are carefully considered, personal preference diminishes, so that the prayer of the community may increase.

As we turn our attention to music's relationships with the paschal mystery and missionary discipleship, then, let us keep those judgments in mind. We will consider those relationships in light of specific musical texts composed for liturgical use. The texts will be a combination of psalms—which comprise "the basic songbook of the Liturgy" (STL, 115b) and "have great power to raise the mind to God" (*General Instruction of the Liturgy of the Hours*, 100)—and hymns, which find their roots in the Liturgy of the Hours, but have also long been used during Mass when "appropriate to the liturgical action" (STL, 115).

Music and the Paschal Mystery

> The human person, though made of body and soul, is a unity. In itself, in its very bodily condition, it synthesizes the elements of the material world, which through it are thus brought to their highest perfection and are enabled to raise their voice in spontaneous praise of the creator. (cf. Col 1:15, *Gaudium et spes*, 14)

Our model for worship—and for all things—is Christ. Fully human and divine, he gave himself completely for us through the paschal mystery of his passion, death, and Resurrection. In *The Ministry of Music*, Kathleen Harmon offers an extended meditation on the relationship between this paschal mystery and liturgical music.[5] Just as Christ gave himself fully, we too must make "the choice to surrender our will to the will of God," which "always requires a dying to self, and emptying of self, a giving of self."[6] Our participation in liturgy is itself a radical ritual participation in the paschal mystery,[7] so when we sing together, we make a kind of "communal surrender" that leads us out of ourselves and facilitates

5. Kathleen Harmon, *The Ministry of Music* (Collegeville, MN: Liturgical Press, 2016), 5–10, 15–16.

6. Harmon, *The Ministry of Music*, 5.

7. Harmon, 6–7.

our rising together as one voice: the Body of Christ at prayer.[8] When pastoral musicians understand this connection between liturgical music and the paschal mystery, they can ensure that the music chosen for liturgy truly facilitates the baptized assembly's dying and rising with Christ.

Liturgically, we celebrate the paschal mystery "within the cycle of a year" (SC, 102), which has both a seasonal cycle (Advent, Christmas, Ordinary Time, Lent, Triduum, Easter, and again Ordinary Time) and a temporal cycle (Marian feasts, saints' days, and other celebrations) that are affixed to particular dates. Liturgical music should be selected in accordance with the rhythm of the liturgical year. Many hymns and chants have come to be associated with specific seasons—"O Come, O Come, Emmanuel" with Advent, scores of carols with Christmas, an often increased use of a cappella music during Lent, and alleluia-filled hymns during Easter. Choosing and staying with a Mass setting for a season also helps the assembly to stay attuned to the progression of the liturgical year. Establishing a seasonal rhythm of music is also important because it corresponds with other seasonal changes in vesture, church environment, and other liturgical symbols to direct the assembly's attention to different dimensions of the paschal mystery.

The liturgical year also provides the framework for the principle of *progressive solemnity*. Music should be selected according to the solemnity of a particular day or occasion, and "not every part that can be sung should necessarily be sung at every celebration" (STL, 115, see also 110–113). Certain seasons such as Advent and Lent call for "a certain musical restraint" (STL, 114), while solemnities and feasts "invite more solemnity" (STL, 113). Following prescribed rubrics and selecting music in accordance with the liturgical year is a foundational means of helping assemblies to give voice to the paschal mystery.

In addition, weddings and funerals provide opportunities to evangelize and catechize the assembly to the relationship between the paschal mystery, Christian Marriage, and Christian death. Well-chosen music draws the assembly into one heart and mind, powerfully communicates the theology of the moment, and rouses the

8. Harmon, 8–10.

spirit. During weddings, this means music should reflect how the "grace of Christian marriage is a fruit of Christ's cross" (CCC, 1615, quoted in STL, 216), while during funerals, it means music "should never be used to memorialize the deceased, but rather to give praise to the Lord, whose Paschal Sacrifice has freed us from the bonds of death" (STL, 248).

Further, at all times, liturgical music has a mystagogical dimension. Catechesis—that is, the "echoing" of the faith—and mystagogy—that is, the living of the "mystery"—are well served when experienced cognitively, kinetically, affectively, spiritually, and musically. Our faith becomes rooted in us when it is embedded into our minds, bodies, hearts, and souls. When we do this repeatedly, the paschal mystery comes to resonate deeply within our being.

Mystagogy is most associated with the period after adults have been initiated into the Church, the period when the newly initiated neophytes reflect more deeply upon the mysteries into which they have been initiated (see RCIA, 244–251). In fact, this period of mystagogy lasts for the entire duration of our lives, and the "entire community" is to reflect together with the neophytes (RCIA, 244). We are continually invited to experience a deeper revelation of Christ and of his paschal mystery, and we are to respond by opening ourselves to receive that revelation—especially when we gather liturgically to celebrate the Eucharist.

The texts that we sing throughout the year should give voice both to this ongoing revelation and to our posture of openness to receiving God's ongoing revelation. Jesse Manibusan's "Open My Eyes" (OCP) echoes the Ephphetha Rite, in which the sign of the cross is traced on various parts of the body with invocations that our eyes, ears, and entire selves may be opened to receiving Christ. David Haas's "Now We Remain" (GIA) recalls that "we remain with Jesus the Christ" because we must continually respond to the call of the paschal mystery: "to live with the Lord, we must die with the Lord." Although most frequently associated with Pentecost, hymns to the Holy Spirit are powerful because they plead with the Spirit to enter our lives and transform us deeply: as in, for example, "Come, Holy Ghost," when we invite the Paraclete to, "in our hearts, take up thy rest." Finally, of course, countless Eucharistic hymns speak of our transformation in light of the paschal mystery. John Schiavone's "Amen, el Cuerpo de Cristo" (OCP) is just one example, a bilingual reminder that "we become what we receive" when "we remember your dying and your rising y contigo Señor resucitamos."[9]

Regardless of whether these or other texts are sung by our liturgical communities, they must be selected carefully. Throughout the course of the liturgical year, music gives voice to our longing to more deeply enter into the paschal mystery and, ultimately, to be one with Christ.

Music and Missionary Discipleship

Liturgical music also prepares us to live as missionary disciples. As Kathleen Harmon describes it, "The gift of that song flows from God to each of us, and from each of us to one another as the Body of Christ, now flows from the Body of Christ to the body of the world." In other words, she says, it "sacramentalizes our mission to the world" (*The Ministry of Music,* 16–17). In *Evangelii gaudium,* Pope Francis exhorts us by declaring, "The Gospel joy which enlivens the community of disciples is a missionary joy" (21). We are called to be "missionary disciples," a people of action—not inaction—and to think of others before we think of ourselves.

Our liturgical music should inspire our assemblies to this life of missionary discipleship: to working for social justice, enacting the preferential option for the poor, and participating in the corporal and spiritual works of mercy. It should direct our attention to how we can serve those who are poor and marginalized. Many psalms do this well, as they remind us of what God does ("hears the cry of the poor," Psalm 34), what God will do ("win justice for the orphaned and oppressed," Psalm 10), and how we are to do the same ("Blessed is the one who is concerned for the poor," Psalm 41). Hymns also remind us of this call to social justice. Willard Jabusch's "Whatsoever You Do" (OCP) paraphrases Jesus' reminder that we "do unto" him when we feed the hungry, visit the imprisoned, and care for "the least of [his] people." Herman Stuempfle's "The Thirsty Cry for Water, Lord" (GIA) pleads with God to "help us also hear the cry of hung'ring, thirsting hearts" and the "risen Christ" will come to us all "that we may rise and live." In addition to these texts,

9. "And with you, Lord, we rise."

contemporary composers continue to be inspired by Scripture (STL, 83) to create new music that directs our attention to the needs of our modern world, thereby contributing to the Church's "ever richer song of her entire gathered people" (STL, 85).

Missionary discipleship also encompasses evangelization; both those who do not know Christ or the Church, and those who do know Christ and his Church, yet need to come to a deeper relationship with him. Many hymns remind us of our call to live the Great Commission and evangelize the world. The familiar hymn, "Lord, You Give the Great Commission," asks that "the Spirit's gifts empower us for the work of ministry"; others echo the dismissal at the end of Mass and tell us to go forth to preach and serve others.[10] These songs seem especially well suited for Ascension, yet throughout the year, they remind us of what it means to live as disciples in the world.

Finally, liturgical music reminds us that missionary discipleship is not optional; as baptized Christians, missionary activity is our duty and our responsibility. In the *Order of the Baptism of Children*, the baptizing minister in the Explanatory Rites says these words as he anoints the child with sacred chrism:

> Almighty God, the Father of our Lord Jesus Christ, / has freed you from sin, / given you new birth by water and the Holy Spirit, / and joined you to his people. / He now anoints you with the Chrism of salvation, / so that you may remain members of Christ, / Priest, Prophet, and King, / unto eternal life. (62)

As missionary disciples, we are called to share in Christ's priestly, prophetic, and kingly ministry. Regardless of our specific musical roles, we share in this ministry through our participation in liturgical music. We exercise our priestly call to be *pray-ers* because whether we sing in the choir, serve as the cantor or the psalmist, play an instrument, or join in the song of the assembly, we do so as disciples at prayer; we *are* pray-ers. We exercise our call to be prophets because as we participate in the song of the Church, we are prophetic witnesses; our raised voices give testimony to the risen Christ. Finally,

---

10 E.g., "Forth in the Peace of Christ We Go" by James Quinn, "Go, Make of All Disciples" by Leon Adkins, "Go Out, Go Out" by Curtis Stephen, and "Go to the World" by Sylvia Dunstan.

we exercise our kingly ministry by humbling ourselves; we lift our voices not for our own glory, but to follow the example of humility that Christ our King has modeled for us.

Being a missionary disciple demands discipline. A disciple is a learner who takes grasp of a belief and lives it. In all of the ways that we have discussed, liturgical music plays an essential role in shaping and disciplining us, thereby helping us to live truly as missionary disciples.

Conclusion

In the 1970s, Fr. Virgil Funk, the founder of National Association of Pastoral Musicians coined the title of "pastoral musician" for those who exercise the ministry of music at the liturgy. Pastoral musicians are to be both musicians and pastors, shepherding the flocks entrusted to their care with love. Ultimately, the pastoral musician's greatest task is helping the assembly to reimagine what it means to be doing "the work of the people." For those who serve as pastoral musicians and liturgists, that means recognizing the importance of liturgical music, ensuring that it helps our assemblies to encounter the paschal mystery more deeply, and reflecting what it means to live as missionary disciples in the world. It means helping them to break their "heart of stone" and aiding them in finding a "heart of flesh" (Ezekiel 36:26).

Through liturgical music, then, the entire Body of Christ affirms its commitment to proclaiming Christ and spreading the Good News that we have received. As *Lumen gentium* says:

> It is therefore quite clear that all Christians in whatever state or walk in life are called to the fullness of Christian life and to the perfection of charity, and this holiness is conducive to a more human way of living even in society here on earth. In order to reach this perfection the faithful should use the strength dealt out to them by Christ's gift, so that, following in his footsteps and conformed to his image, doing the will of God in everything, they may wholeheartedly devote themselves to the glory of God and to the service of their neighbor. Thus the holiness of the people of God will grow in fruitful abundance. . . . (40)

At its best, liturgical music does precisely what all liturgy does: it opens us to an encounter with the living God, inspires ourselves to recognize and be open to God's work in us, and helps us to grow in holiness, all so that we will go forth and share God's grace and mercy with the world.

Questions for Discussion:

1. Think about a time when music has really moved your heart to a deeper understanding of the paschal mystery. What about the music inspired that movement and that transformation?
2. Select a musical piece at random. Would it pass the liturgical, pastoral, and musical judgements? When would it be appropriate for use in the liturgy? When not?
3. How do you hear the call to be a missionary disciple through liturgical music? Has it caused you to have a change of direction in your life?

BIBLIOGRAPHY

Benedict XVI. *Meeting with Artists: Address of His Holiness Benedict XVI* .November 21, 2009. Accessed December 9, 2019. http://www.vatican.va/content/benedict-xvi/en/speeches/2009/november/documents/hf_ben-xvi_spe_20091121_artisti.html.

———. *Sacramentum caritatis.* Washington, DC: United States Conference of Catholic Bishops, 2007.

Beraudy, SS, Roger. *Scrutinies and Exorcisms.* Vol. 22 of *Adult Baptism and the Catechumenate,* edited by Johannes Wagner, 57–61. New York /Glen Rock, NJ: Paulist Press, 1967.

Brown, SJ, Joseph A. *To Stand on the Rock: Meditations on Black Catholic Identity.* Maryknoll, NY: Orbis Books, 1988.

Burghardt, SJ, Walter J. 1999. "Just Word and Just Worship: Biblical Justice and Christian Worship." *Workship* 73, no. 5.

Catholic Church. *Catechism of the Catholic Church.* 2nd ed. Washington, DC: United States Conference of Catholic Bishops, 2000.

———. *Order of Baptism of Children.* Translated by ICEL. Chicago: Liturgy Training Publications, 2020.

———. *Rite of Christian Initiation of Adults: Study Edition.* Translated by ICEL. Chicago: Liturgy Training Publications, 1988.

———. *The General Instruction of the Roman Missal.* Translated by ICEL. Washington, DC: United States Conference of Catholic Bishops, 2010.

Cervers, OCD, Jesus Castellano. "Liturgy and Spirituality." In *The Handbook for Liturgical Studies,* vol. 2, *Fundamental Liturgy,* edited by Anscar Chupungo, OSB. Collegeville, MN: Liturgical Press, 1997.

Chauvet, Louis-Marie. *The Sacraments: The World of God at the Mercy of the Body.* Translated by Madeleine Beaumont. Collegeville, MN: Liturgical Press, 2001.

Collins, Patrick. *Bodying Forth: Aesthetic Liturgy.* New York/Mahwah, NJ: Paulist Press, 1992.

Cones, Bryan, and Robert Taft. "Mass Instruction: Fr. Robert Taft on Liturgical Reform." *U.S. Catholic* 74, no. 12 (December 2009): 29.

Congregation for the Clergy. *General Directory for Catechesis.* Washington, DC: United States Conference of Catholic Bishops, 1998.

Congregation of Rites. 1967. *Musicam sacram.* March 5. Accessed December 9, 2019. http://www.vatican.va/archive/hist_councils/ii_vatican_council/documents/vat-ii_instr_19670305_musicam-sacram_en.html.

Donahue, SJ, John R. "Biblical Perspectives on Justice." In *The Faith that Does Justice,* edited by John C. Haughey. New York: Paulist Press, 1977.

Editors. "From the Catholic Worker." Edited by Virgil Michel. *Orate Fratres* 8, no. 6 (1934).

Ferrone, Rita. "Scrutiny, Exorcism, and the Construction of the Christian Self." Edited by Mary Fox. *Catechumenate* 33, no. 1 (2011).

Ford, Paul F. "Lived Liturgy, First Spirituality." *Liturgical Ministry* 10 (2001): 186.

Francis. *Address of His Holiness Pope Francis to Participants in the Plenary Assembly of the Pontifical Committee for International Eucharistic Congresses.* November 10, 2018. Accessed December 9, 2019. http://w2.vatican.va/content/francesco/en/speeches/2018/november/documents.

———. *Apostolic Exhortation on the Joy of the Gospel (Evangelii Gaudium).* Washington, DC: United States Conference of Catholic Bishops, 2016.

Harmon, SNDDEN, Kathleen. *The Ministry of Music.* Collegeville, MN: Liturgical Press, 2016.

Himes, Michael J. *The Mystery of Faith: An Introduction to Catholicism.* Cincinnati: Franciscan Media, 2004.

Hughes, RSCJ, Kathleen. *Saying Amen: A Mystagogy of Sacrament*. Chicago: Liturgy Training Publications, 1999.

John Paul II. *Letter to Artists*. April 4, 1999. Accessed December 9, 2019. http://www.vatican.va/content/john-paul-ii/en/letters/1999/documents/hf_jp-ii_let_23041999_artists.html.

———. *Dies Domini: On Keeping the Lord's Day Holy*. Boston: Pauline Books and Media, 1998.

Joncas, J. Michael. *Preaching the Rites of Christian Initiation*. Chicago: Liturgy Training Publications, 1994.

Kavanagh, OSB, Aidan. *On Liturgical Theology*. Collegeville, MN: Liturgical Press, 1984.

———. *The Shape of Baptism: The Rite of Christian Initiation*. Collegeville, MN: Liturgical Press, 1978.

Michel, OSB, Virgil. "The Basics of Social Regeneration." *Orate Fratres* 9, no. 12 (1935).

Miller, David. "Justice." *The Stanford Encyclopedia of Philosophy*. Fall 2017 Edition, edited by Edward N. Zalta. October 4, 2019. https://plato.stanford.edu/archives/fall2017/entries/justice/.

Paul VI. *Evangelii nuntiandi*. December 8, 1975. Accessed December 9, 2019. http://www.vatican.va/content/paul-vi/en/apost_exhortations/documents/hf_p-vi_exh_19751208_evangelii-nuntiandi.html.

Pius X. *Tra le sollecitudini*. November 22, 1903. Accessed December 9, 2019. https://adoremus.org/1903/11/22/tra-le-sollecitudini/.

Pius XI. *Quadragesimo anno*. May 15, 1931. Accessed December 9, 2019. http://www.vatican.va/content/pius-xi/en/encyclicals/documents/hf_p-xi_enc_19310515_quadragesimo-anno.html.

Power, OMI, David. "Eucharistic Justice." *Theological Studies* 67, no. 4 (2006).

Rahner, SJ, Karl. *The Trinity*. Translated by Jospeh Donceel. London: Burns and Oates, 1975.

Regan, CSSR, David. *Experience the Mystery: Pastoral Possibilities for Christian Mystagogy.* Collegeville, MN: Liturgical Press, 1994.

Roll, Susan. "The Concluding Rites: Theology of the Latin Text and Rite." In *A Commentary on the Order of the Mass of the The Roman Missal,* edited by Edward Foley, OFM. Collegeville, MN: Liturgical Press, 2011.

Rouet, Albert. *Liturgy and the Arts.* Translated by Paul Philibert, OP. Collegeville, MN: Liturgical Press, 1997.

Satterlee, Craig A. *Ambrose of Milan's Method of Mystagogical Preaching.* Collegeville, MN: Liturgical Press, 2002.

Searle, Mark. "Serving the Lord with Justice." In *Liturgy and Social Justice,* edited by Mark Searle. Collegeville, MN: Liturgical Press, 1980.

Second Vatican Council. "Decree on the Apostolate of Lay People *Apostolicam actuositatem.*" In *Vatican Council II: The Basic Sixteen Documents,* edited by Austin Flanner, OP. Collegeville, MN: Liturgical Press, 2014.

———. "Decree on the Church's Missionary Activity *Ad gentes divinitus.*" In *Vatican Council II: The Basic Sixteen Documents,* edited by Austin Flanner, OP. Collegeville, MN: Liturgical Press, 2014.

———. "Dogmatic Constitution on the Church *Lumen gentium.*" In *Vatican Council II: The Basic Sixteen Documents,* edited by Austin Flanner, OP. Collegeville, MN: Liturgical Press, 2014.

———. "Pastoral Constitution on the Church in the Modern World *Gaudium et spes.*" In *Vatican Council II: The Basic Sixteen Documents,* edited by Austin Flanner, OP. Collegeville, MN: Liturgical Press, 2014.

———. *Sacrosanctum concilium.* In *Documents on the Liturgy, 1963–1979: Conciliar, Papal, and Curial Texts,* translated by ICEL. Collegeville, MN: Liturgical Press, 1982.

Smith, Gregory A. *Just One-Third of Catholics Agree with Their Church that Eucharist Is Body, Blood of Christ.* Pew Research Center, August 5, 2019. https://www.pewresearch.org/fact-tank/2019/08/05/transubstantiation-eucharist-u-s-catholics/.

Tkacik, Michael J. "Eucharist and Liturgy as Means to Social Justice in Vatican II." *Social Justice Review* 92, no. 5/6 (2001).

United States Conference of Catholic Bishops. *Economic Justice for All: Pastoral Letter on Catholic Social Teaching and the U.S. Economy.* Washington, DC: United States Conference of Catholic Bishops, 1986.

———. *Go and Make Disciples: A National Plan and Strategy for Catholic Evangelization in the United States.* Washington, DC: United States Conference of Catholic Bishops, 2002.

———. *Sing to the Lord: Music in Divine Worship.* Washington, DC: United States Conference of Catholic Bishops, 2007.

Wedig, OP, Mark E. "Evangelization, Inculturation, and the RCIA." *Worship* 76, no. 6 (2002).

Wickes, Mariette. "Discussion." *1956 North American Liturgical Week Proceedings: People's Participation and Holy Week.* The Liturgical Conference, 1957.

Yarnold, SJ, Edward. *The Awe-Inspiring Rites of Initiation.* Collegeville, MN: Liturgical Press, 1994.

Zizioulas, John. *Being as Communion.* Crestwood, NY: St. Vladimir's Seminary Press, 1997.

CONTRIBUTORS

Michael S. Driscoll is professor emeritus of sacramental and liturgical theology and the founding director of the masters program in sacred music at the University of Notre Dame. A graduate of the Université Paris-Sorbonne, Paris IV, and the Institut Catholique de Paris, he is the author of "Eucharist and Justice," in *Sacraments and Justice* (Liturgical Press, 2014) and coauthor of *The Order of Mass: A Roman Missal Study Edition and Workbook* (2011) from Liturgy Training Publications. His current research is in the area of liturgy and aesthetics and the connection between Eucharist and ethics.

Katharine E. Harmon is assistant professor of theology and a private instructor in organ at Marian University in Indianapolis. A graduate of the University of Notre Dame, she is the author of *There Were Also Many Woman There: Lay Women in the Liturgical Movement in the United States, 1926–1959* (2013) from Liturgical Press. Her writing has also appeared in *Worship, American Catholic Studies, Studia Liturgica,* and *Empowering the People of God: Catholic Action Before and After Vatican II* (Fordham University Press, 2013). She serves as a pastoral musician at St. Mark the Evangelist in Indianapolis.

Christian McConnell is the director of the Institute for Ongoing Formation and assistant professor of liturgy and sacramental theology at St. Peter's Seminary in London, Ontario. He is a graduate of the University of Notre Dame. He was an editor of and contributing author to *A Living Tradition: On the Intersection of Liturgical History and Pastoral Practice, Essays in Honor of Maxwell E. Johnson* (Liturgical Press, 2012). His article, "Timing Midnight Mass," appeared in *Pastoral Liturgy* vol. 38, no. 5 (LTP, 2007).

Anne McGowan is assistant professor of liturgy at Catholic Theological Union in Chicago. A graduate of the University of Notre Dame, she is the author of *Eucharistic Epicleses, Ancient and Modern* (2014) and coauthor of *The Pilgrimage of Egeria: A New Translation of the "Itinerarium Egeriae" with Introduction and Commentary* (2018), both from Liturgical Press. She and her husband, Patrick McGowan, are raising two young children.

Rodica Stoicoiu is an independent scholar and director of liturgy at St.Agnes Parish, Shepherdstown, WV. A graduate of the Catholic University of America and the University of Notre Dame, she has contributed book chapters to *Genesis, Evolution and the Search for a Reasoned Faith* (Anselm Academic, 2011), *Eucharist and Social Justice in the Heart of Catholic Social Justice* (Brazos Press, 2009), *Where Justice and Mercy Meet: Catholic Opposition to the Death Penalty* (Liturgical Press, 2013), and *Catholic Sacraments: A Rich Source of Blessings* (Paulist Press, 2015). She has written numerous articles and columns in publications like *Liturgical Ministry* and *New Theological Review.* She has taught at both the graduate and undergraduate levels. Her current research interests are in the areas of Roman Catholic-Orthodox dialogue and the theology of liturgy, especially as this informs the theology of Eucharist, Church, and ministry.

Eric T. Styles is the rector of Carroll Hall, an undergraduate residential community at the University of Notre Dame. With degrees from the University of Cincinnati and Loyola University Chicago, he has worked in parish and college liturgy, faith formation, and Ignatian spirituality. He has written for *America Magazine* and *Church Life Journal*, particularly interested in the intersections of liturgy, culture, and the arts. A characteristic piece called "Black Bodies, Kneeling, and the Liturgy" was written for CLJ in October of 2017.

Mark E. Wedig, OP, is a Dominican friar from the Southern Province of St. Martin de Porres and a graduate of the Catholic University of America. He currently serves as president of the Aquinas Institute of Theology in St. Louis where he is also professor of liturgical and sacramental theology. He has published many articles including "Ecclesial Architecture and Image in a Postmodern Age" in *Transcending Architecture: Contemporary Views on Sacred Space* (Catholic University Press, 2015), "Ritual: Celebrating Faith and Belief" in *Theology: Faith, Beliefs and Traditions* (Kendall Hunt Publishing, 2009), and "The Eucharist: A Mystery to Be Celebrated: Full Participation in the Liturgical Action" in *Pastoral Liturgy* vol. 39, no. 4 (LTP, 2008).

Fabian R. Yanez is the executive secretary for the Southwest Liturgical Conference and the former director of the Office of Worship for the Archdiocese of Santa Fe in New Mexico, former director of liturgy and music for Light of the World Catholic Parish in Littleton, Colorado, and former director of the Office of Liturgy for the Diocese of Belleville in Illinois. He is a graduate of St. Joseph's College in Rensselaer, Indiana, a graduate of Avila College in Kansas City, Missouri, and studied at the Conservatory of Music at the University of Missouri–Kansas City. He resides in Denver, Colorado, with his wife, Delaine.